Sandra Lee

Bake Sale Cookbook

This book belongs to:

_____

Angel Cupcake Minis, *page 164*

The Sound of Sweets
(Party Playlist)

1. Pure Imagination - Gene Wilder
2. Sugar, Sugar - The Archies
3. Happy Days - Norman Gimbel & Charles Fox
4. Barbie Girl - Aqua
5. How Sweet It Is - Marvin Gaye
6. I Want Candy - Bow Wow Wow
7. Lollipop - The Chordettes
8. Oompa Loompa - Oompa Loompa Cast
9. Somewhere Over the Rainbow - Judy Garland
10. Sugar Baby Love - The Rubettes
11. The Candy Man - Aubrey Woods
12. Fireflies - Owl City
13. Girl's Just Want to Have Fun - Cyndi Lauper

PARTY PERFECT ICE CREAM TREAT

Marble Slab Creamery® has the best-ever ice cream combination. Mix together Sweet Cream Ice Cream, chocolate sprinkles, mint patties, and fudge topping. They call this creation Memorial Day Madness. I call it incredible.

For general information on our other products and services or for technical support, please contact our Customer Care Department within the United States at (800) 762-2974, outside the United States at (317) 572-3993, or fax (317) 572-4002.

Wiley also publishes its books in a variety of electronic formats. Some content that appears in print may not be available in electronic books. For more information about Wiley products, visit our web site at www.wiley.com.

Library of Congress Cataloging-in-Publication Data:
Lee, Sandra, 1966-
    Sandra Lee bake sale cookbook/Sandra Lee.
        p. cm.
    Includes index.
    ISBN 978-0-470-64559-8 (pbk.)
    1. Baking. 2. Desserts. 3. Pastry. 4. Cooking, American. 5. Cookbooks.
I. Title. II. Bake sale cookbook.
    TX765.L45 2011
    641.8'15--dc22

                                                    2010036855

Printed in the United States of America.

10 9 8 7 6 5 4 3 2 1

SL BOOKS
sandralee.com

WILEY
John Wiley & Sons, Inc.

Get our Magazine

Find scrumptious bake-sale treats and glorious cakes to grace your tablescapes. Every issue is filled with quick-and-easy recipes for all your baking needs.

Brilliant Bakes

Every issue includes fabulous shortcut sweets with a semi-homemade secret. These easy baked desserts will impress eyes and sweet tooths alike.

Sweet Socials

Gather those dear to you, and celebrate life's most special moments—birthdays, showers, and parties—with a dessert buffet filled with yummy confections.

Cupcakes and Cookies You'll Love

Bring sunny smiles to your friends and family with freshly baked cookies galore and moist cupcakes slathered with sweet frosting.

Seasonal Sweets

Budget-friendly hints and tips help you create seasonal sweets to suit every holiday theme, from classic Christmas cookies to ghoulish Halloween goodies.

Bake Sale Theme Ideas

January: New Year's, Chinese New Year, National Pie Day (January 23)

February: National Chocolate Month, National Cake Month, Valentine's Day

March: First Day of Spring (March 21), St. Patrick's Day, Mardi Gras

April: Easter, Earth Day, April Fool's Day

May: May Day, Mother's Day, Cinco de Mayo

June: National Candy Month, Father's Day, National Dairy Month

July: National Ice Cream Month, Fourth of July, National Blueberry Month

August: Friendship Day (first Sunday), Back-to-School, National KidsDay (August 7)

September: Hunger Action Month, Labor Day, Peace Day (September 21)

October: National Pumpkin Month, Halloween, National Cookie Month

November: Thanksgiving, Harvestfest, World Kindness Day (November 13)

December: Christmas, Hanukkah, National Cupcake Day (December 15)

The Sweet Things in Life

Few things in life are as sweet as making your friends and family something wonderfully sensational from your own kitchen. The smell that fills your home is second only to the sweetness that fills your heart and soul when your loved ones enjoy what you've made.

Bake sales are not just for children—they're for the kid in all of us. A bake sale should include plenty of sweet treats, but it is equally important to have some savory eats. Make the most of the moment and set a bake sale table brimming with all the enchantment your inner child can create.

Bake sales are also a brilliant fund-raising idea. Just think, with the whirl of your whisk, you can change lives any time of year. Throw a bake sale for Share Our Strength®, an organization that helps feed more than 17 million kids in America who would go hungry every day without your support. If you go to strength.org and click on the Great American Bake Sale link, you can join me in ending childhood hunger in America. So grab some friends, some coworkers, some church or community members and go to town with your bake sale. You'll have so much fun and you'll make a huge difference in a child's life.

I would like to thank the many partners and friends who have helped me bring awareness to the most worthy cause of ending childhood hunger in America: Share Our Strength®, No Kid Hungry™, Feeding America®, our nation's food banks, Domino® and C&H® sugars, Duncan Hines®, Valpak®, Pyrex®, Marble Slab Creamery®, the team from the *Semi-Homemade* Magazine, *Family Circle®, Better Homes and Gardens®*, and my entire Food Network family—thank you! And thank you, Semi-Homemakers. May God bless you with every wonderful thing.

Enjoy and cheers to a happy, healthy home,

Sandra Lee

Table of Contents

Chapter 1 | Creative Cakes 22

For celebrations and special days of all kinds—birthdays, Mother's Day, anniversaries, homecomings, and more—baking a homemade cake for someone you love is a sweet, thoughtful—and always appreciated—way to show you care.

Chapter 2 | Cupcake Craze 42

These little cakes for one are no longer just for children's birthday parties—grown-ups want in on the fun too! This collection includes cupcakes that are both whimsical and sophisticated—and sure to bring on the smiles.

Chapter 3 | Cookies, Cookies 62

Cookies are always a big hit at bake sales because they're so versatile—they have nearly limitless tastes and textures. Bake up a batch or two to fill the cookie jar, serve as dessert, or package prettily to give as gifts.

Table of Contents

Easy-on-the-baker bars and brownies (just mix, pour, bake, and cut!) are among the simplest baked goods to make for any occasion. A square of something sweet to eat with coffee, tea, or a glass of milk is always a welcome treat.

These speedy treats take advantage of high-quality prepared ingredients and a few clever tricks to turn out sweets that look and taste as if they took all day to make—perfect for drop-in dinner guests and spur-of-the-moment fundraisers!

Sometimes nothing hits the sweet spot like the taste of a familiar spice cake, jam-filled cookie, or coconut-topped brownie. These are the flavors food memories are built on, and fortunately, they just grow sweeter with time.

Table of Contents

Chapter 7 | Fruit Fête 122

A piece of fresh fruit may be the simplest dessert, but dressing it up with sugar, butter, or chocolate only enhances the beauty and taste! For any season or reason, serve these fruit-centered desserts warm, cold—or, sometimes, with ice cream.

Chapter 8 | Chocolate Decadence 136

There are many times—for a romantic dinner, Valentine's Day bake sale, or girls' night in—when only the rich, luxurious taste of chocolate will do. Indulge in cocoa-infused treats such as truffles, tarts, cheesecake, and more.

Chapter 9 | Candied Creations 152

Show your affection with a homemade confection! The hand-crafted candies and other bite-size goodies in this collection may be small, but they deliver big impact for taste and prettiness. Small packages of little treats are big sellers.

Table of Contents

Chapter 10 | Pies & Pastries 170

Topped with fresh seasonal fruit, rich cheesecake, light-as-air mousse, or creamy custard, a flaky pastry or crumbly cookie crust has undeniable appeal. Fill a buttery crust with something delicious and customers will line up for a slice.

Chapter 11 | American Fair 190

Some goodies appear at bake sales and potlucks all across America. Put any of these traditional treats—including Apple-Cranberry Crumble, Lousiana Mudslide Pie, and Rocky Road Parfaits—on the table and they'll disappear in a flash.

Chapter 12 | Cookiescapes 212

Sheer fun is part of the process of making these stunning arrangements. Convenience products and simple tricks make them surprisingly easy to make as gifts, centerpieces, and bake sale items. Eat them or simply admire them.

Basics

Make baked goods taste and look even better by filling, frosting, embellishing, and packaging them.

Filled

Frosted

Embellished

Savory

Packaged

Cream Cheese Icing
and Golden Frosting

Frosted

The practical reason to frost or ice baked goods is to keep them from drying out. But frosting also adds flavor, color, texture, and shape to cakes, cookies, and bars. For some, it's the best part of dessert.

Cream Cheese Icing In a mixing bowl, beat 1 pound cream cheese, softened; 1 stick butter, softened; 2 cups powdered sugar; and 2 teaspoons vanilla extract until light and fluffy. It can be left white—as on the cookies on page 12—or tinted with food coloring.

Golden Frosting In a mixing bowl, beat 1 (16-ounce) can vanilla frosting, 1/4 cup dulce de leche, and 1/4 to 1/2 cup powdered sugar until thick and spreadable. To get the textured effect shown on the cake on page 12, spread a thick layer of frosting on the top of the cake. Press the back of a spoon into the frosting, turning the spoon slightly as you lift it.

Maple Pumpkin Glaze Combine 1 cup powdered sugar and 1 teaspoon pumpkin pie spice. Beat in 1 tablespoon maple syrup and 1/4 cup heavy cream until thick yet pourable.

Caramel Frosting In a cold mixing bowl, beat 2 cups chilled heavy cream with a hand mixer almost until soft peaks form. Add 1 1/2 cans dulce de leche (13.4 ounces each) and beat until well blended and soft peaks form. A dollop of this light but rich frosting is delicious on brownies.

Simple Poured Icing In a mixing bowl, combine 2 cups powdered sugar and enough lemon juice (1 to 2 tablespoons) to form a thin glaze. Use this simplest of all glazes to dress up a purchased angel food cake, as it does here, or a Bundt cake. It can be used white or tinted with liquid food coloring.

Maple Pumpkin Glaze

Caramel Frosting

Simple Poured Icing

Filled

It's a special treat to find a sweet surprise in a cookie, cupcake, or slice of cake. Fillings don't have to be complicated. You can use lemon curd or any flavor of frosting, pudding, jam, or preserves.

Custard-Filled Cake Boxed pudding and pie filling makes a lovely creamy filling for layer cakes. Good flavor choices include vanilla, lemon, chocolate, and banana cream. Leave at least a $\frac{1}{2}$-inch border so the filling doesn't squish out when you stack the top layer. For a grown-up cake, sprinkle a tablespoon or two of rum or orange or coffee-flavored liqueur before spreading on the custard. Be sure to refrigerate a custard-filled cake until serving time.

Filled Cupcakes Whipped frosting in a pastry bag works beautifully for filling cupcakes. After the cupcakes have cooled, insert a large star tip into the bottom of the cupcake and gently squeeze. Work quickly—your hands will warm the frosting and it will melt into the cake if you're not careful.

Heavenly Angel Food Cake The channel method is the best way to fill an angel food cake. First, cut the cake in half horizontally with a serrated knife. Using a small knife, cut a channel in the center of the bottom layer, being careful not to cut all the way through cake bottom. Fill the channel with pudding or custard, replace the top layer, and frost or glaze the entire cake as desired.

Sandwich Cookies With a filling, almost any cookie can be a doubly delicious sandwich cookie. A popular combination, shown here, is lemon curd with ginger cookies. Just be sure that any cookies you use are thin enough so that the sandwich you create isn't too big to eat!

15

Embellished

Make your baked goods stand out from the crowd. Even the simplest decorations—chocolate curls, colored sugar, and sprinkles—make eye-catching (and customer-fetching) cakes, cookies, and cupcakes.

Chocolate Curls Curlicues of chocolate add an elegant touch to cakes and cupcakes. Simply pull a vegetable peeler along the narrow end of a large bar of milk chocolate (milk chocolate is softer than dark chocolate, so it curls easily). Hold the bar in the wrapper or in a piece of waxed paper to avoid melting chocolate on your fingers. If the bar is too hard, just hold it for a minute or two; the warmth from your hand should soften it enough to make it easy to shave.

Basic Chocolate Icing Heat 1 cup heavy cream over low heat until simmering. Remove from heat and stir in 8 ounces of chocolate chips until melted and smooth. Use while warm. This icing is perfect for dipping or drizzling.

Sprinkles, Edible Pearls, and More Purchased candy buttons, sprinkles, edible pearls, and frosting flowers give baked goods instant impact. Or get creative with candy. Here, chopped thin mints add beauty and flavor to a chocolate cupcake.

Colored Sugars This is the simplest way to add sparkle to a cookie. I like to use tone-on-tone frosting and sugar colors (blue sugar on blue frosting, green sugar on green frosting, and so on). Decorating sugars come in a variety of hues and textures—from fine to coarse to pearl sugar. You can also make your own by placing ½ cup of white granulated *Domino*®/ *C&H*® sugar and a few drops of food coloring in a plastic bag. Shake and work coloring through sugar until desired hue is reached. Spread colored sugar on a baking sheet until dry.

Savory

As an alternative to the sugar, take savory items to your next bake sale, put on an all-savory bake sale—or even host a lunch bake sale.

Savory Cheese Palmiers Sprinkle work surface with grated Parmesan cheese. Unfold a thawed sheet of puff pastry on top of cheese. Brush pastry with egg wash made from 1 egg beaten with 1 tablespoon water. Combine 2 tablespoons Parmesan cheese, ¼ cup shredded Italian cheese blend, and 1 teaspoon paprika. Sprinkle over surface. Press into pastry. Fold top and bottom edge of pastry to center. Fold pastry in half from left to right. Fold in half top to bottom. Cover and refrigerate 30 minutes. Cut ⅛-inch-thick slices, starting at shortest edge. Dip flat faces of Palmiers in Parmesan; lay on baking sheet. Bake in a 400°F oven for 20 minutes.

Soft Pretzels Divide a thawed loaf of bread dough into 14 pieces. Roll each piece into a 16-inch rope and form into a pretzel shape. Cover and refrigerate. Bring 4 quarts of water to a boil. Boil pretzels, 3 at a time, until they rise to the surface. Drain on paper towels. Arrange 3 inches apart on a buttered sheet pan. Brush with a beaten egg and sprinkle with coarse salt or finely grated Parmesan cheese and garlic powder. Bake in a 400°F oven for 15 minutes or until brown.

Pizza Squares Top a bread shell with your favorite toppings, bake, then cut into small squares.

Pigs in a Blanket Cut buttermilk biscuits into 6 pieces each. Roll each dough ball in shredded cheddar cheese. Wrap around cooked small beef sausages. Bake on a parchment-lined baking sheet in a 375°F oven for 10 minutes.

Packaged

Putting the final touch on bake sale goods is a matter of putting them in something protective and pretty. Just a little bit of color from a satiny ribbon works magic on even the humblest pie.

All Wrapped Up Cellophane bags of all sizes—clear, colored, and patterned—are sold at crafts stores. Use large ones to package unfrosted cakes and coffee cakes, and small ones for cookies and cupcakes. Tie the bags with pretty multicolored and patterned ribbons.

Bountiful Buckets Pile cookies in decorative tin pails found at crafts stores. You can place the filled pails in a cellophane bag tied with a ribbon as well, if you like. Or, for a more rustic look, use small disposable aluminum baking pans lined with colorful tissue paper (see Banana-Cashew Cookies on page 67).

Simple Sacks Inexpensive and colorful gift bags are an extremely easy way to package cookies for a bake sale. Line the bags with tissue paper or not. Add a price tag and you're set.

Tea Party Package Petit fours in pastel icing or tiny tea cookies are perfectly proportioned for filling a china tea cup. Look at yard sales and secondhand stores for the cups—then you can sell the cup and saucer and goodies as a package deal. If you or someone you know is a coffee drinker, see the packaging idea for Cappuccino Fudge Cupcakes on page 45.

Baker's Dozen You'll be most successful at any bake sale if you offer an array of package sizes for your baked goods. After all, some people are looking for a single treat to have right then with a cup of coffee, while others are looking for a cake to take to a party.

Creative Cakes

Nothing says "special occasion" as clearly as a cake. Baking a cake for someone you love is a sweet, thoughtful—and always appreciated—way to show you care.

White Chocolate Macadamia Cake

Prep 30 minutes   **Bake** 32 minutes   **Cool** 35 minutes   **Oven** 350°F   **Makes** 10 servings

Nonstick cooking spray

1   **package (18.25 ounces) white cake mix**, *Duncan Hines®*

1   **package (4-serving-size) instant white chocolate pudding and pie filling mix**, *Jell-O®*

⅔   **cup refrigerated liquid egg whites**, *All Whites®*

½   **cup light coconut milk**, *A Taste of Thai®*

½   **cup vegetable oil**

1   **cup white baking chips**, *Nestlé®*

1¼   **cups chopped macadamia nuts**, *Diamond of California®*

2   **containers (12 ounces each) whipped cream cheese frosting**, *Duncan Hines®*

1. Preheat oven to 350°F. Spray two 8-inch round cake pans with cooking spray; set aside.

2. In a large mixing bowl, combine cake mix and pudding mix. Add egg whites, coconut milk, and oil. Beat with an electric mixer on low for 30 seconds. Scrape down the side of bowl; beat on medium for 1 minute more. Batter will be thick. Stir in white baking chips and ½ cup of the chopped macadamia nuts. Spread into prepared pans.

3. Bake for 32 to 35 minutes or until a toothpick inserted near centers comes out clean. Cool in pans on a wire rack for 10 minutes; remove from pans. Cool completely on wire rack.

4. For macadamia nut frosting, in a medium bowl, stir together ½ cup of the remaining chopped macadamia nuts and one container of the cream cheese frosting.

5. To assemble, place one cake layer on a serving plate. Spread with macadamia nut frosting; top with the second cake layer. Frost entire cake with the remaining cream cheese frosting. Garnish with the remaining ¼ cup macadamia nuts.

Black Russian Cake

Prep 25 minutes   **Bake** 25 minutes   **Cool** 35 minutes   **Oven** 350°F   **Makes** 10 servings

Nonstick cooking spray

1   package (19.5 ounces) dark chocolate cake mix, *Duncan Hines*®

1   package (4-serving-size) instant chocolate pudding and pie filling mix, *Jell-O*®

¾   cup chocolate milk, *Nesquik*®

½   cup vegetable oil

3   eggs

6   tablespoons cream soda

5   tablespoons strong-brewed coffee

2   teaspoons vanilla extract, *McCormick*®

2   containers (12 ounces each) whipped chocolate frosting, *Duncan Hines*®

1   bar (1.45 ounces) dark chocolate, finely grated, *Hershey's*® *Special Dark*

1. Preheat oven to 350°F. Spray two 8-inch round cake pans with cooking spray; set aside.

2. In a large mixing bowl, combine cake mix and pudding mix. Add chocolate milk, oil, eggs, cream soda, 1 tablespoon of the coffee, and vanilla extract. Beat with an electric mixer on low for 30 seconds. Scrape down side of bowl; beat on medium for 2 minutes more. Pour batter into prepared pans.

3. Bake for 25 to 30 minutes or until a toothpick inserted near centers comes out clean. Cool in pans on a wire rack for 10 minutes; remove from pans. Cool completely on wire rack.

4. In a medium bowl, stir together the remaining ¼ cup coffee and the frosting.

5. To assemble, place a cake layer on a serving plate. Spread with ½ cup of the frosting mixture; top with the second cake layer. Frost side and top with the remaining frosting. Lightly press grated chocolate onto side of cake.

Opera Cake

Prep 35 minutes   **Bake** 25 minutes   **Cool** 35 minutes   **Oven** 350°F   **Makes** 12 servings

Nonstick cooking spray

1   package (18.25 ounces) yellow cake mix, *Duncan Hines®*

1   cup milk

½   cup (1 stick) butter, softened

3   eggs

2   teaspoons almond extract, *McCormick®*

½   cup almonds, ground, *Planters®*

3½   cups semisweet chocolate chips, *Nestle®*

2   cups heavy cream

2   tablespoons light-color corn syrup, *Karo®*

2   tablespoons espresso powder

1   container (12 ounces) whipped buttercream frosting, *Betty Crocker®*

Unsweetened cocoa powder, *Hershey's®*

Chocolate decorating icing, *Betty Crocker® Easy Flow*

1. Preheat oven to 350°F. Generously spray three 8-inch square baking pans with cooking spray; set aside.

2. In a large mixing bowl, beat cake mix, milk, butter, eggs, and almond extract with an electric mixer on low for 30 seconds. Scrape down the side of bowl; beat on medium for 2 minutes more. Stir in almonds. Pour batter into prepared pans.

3. Bake for 25 to 30 minutes or until a toothpick inserted near centers comes out clean. Cool in pans on wire racks for 15 minutes; carefully remove pans. Cool completely on wire racks.

4. Meanwhile, place chocolate chips in a medium microwave-safe bowl; set aside. In a small saucepan, heat cream and corn syrup over medium heat until nearly boiling. Pour mixture over chocolate chips, stirring until mixture is smooth. Cool until a spreadable consistency.

5. For espresso-buttercream frosting, stir espresso powder into buttercream frosting until combined; set aside.

6. To assemble, place one cake layer on a serving plate. Stir espresso-buttercream frosting; spread half the frosting on cake layer. Spread one-fourth of the chocolate mixture over buttercream; top with another cake layer. Repeat with the remaining espresso-buttercream frosting, another one-fourth of the chocolate mixture, and the remaining cake layer.

7. Microwave the remaining chocolate mixture on medium about 30 seconds or until chocolate is a thick but pourable consistency. Pour chocolate over top of cake, spreading down the side. Dust half the cake top with cocoa powder. Using decorating icing, pipe a squiggle diagonally across the cake and pipe a border around the bottom edge of the cake.

Cupcake Cake

Prep 35 minutes   **Bake** 25 minutes + 45 minutes   **Cool** 35 minutes   **Oven** 350°F   **Makes** 24 servings

Nonstick cooking spray

1   **package (18.25 ounces) yellow cake mix,** *Duncan Hines*®

1   **cup all-purpose flour**

1   **cup milk**

8   **eggs**

1   **cup sour cream**

⅓   **cup plus ½ cup vegetable oil**

1   **teaspoon vanilla extract,** *McCormick*®

1   **package (18.25 ounces) chocolate cake mix,** *Duncan Hines*®

¼   **cup unsweetened cocoa powder,** *Hershey's*®

1⅓   **cups chocolate milk,** *Nesquik*®

2   **containers (12 ounces each) whipped chocolate frosting,** *Duncan Hines*®

1   **container (12 ounces) whipped buttercream frosting,** *Betty Crocker*®

    Assorted jelly beans, *Jelly Belly*®

    Pastel confetti sprinkles

1. Preheat oven to 350°F. Generously spray two 8-inch round cake pans and one 8-inch-diameter ovenproof bowl with cooking spray; set aside. Line six 2½-inch muffin cups with paper baking cups; set aside.

2. In a large mixing bowl, combine yellow cake mix and ½ cup of the flour. Add milk, 4 of the eggs, ½ cup of the sour cream, the ⅓ cup oil, and the vanilla extract. Beat with an electric mixer on low for 30 seconds. Scrape down the side of bowl; beat on medium for 2 minutes more. Pour batter into prepared cake pans.

3. Bake for 25 to 30 minutes or until toothpick inserted near centers comes out clean. Cool in pans on a wire rack for 10 minutes; remove from pans. Cool completely on wire rack.

4. In another large bowl, combine chocolate cake mix, the remaining ½ cup flour, and the cocoa powder. Add chocolate milk, the remaining 4 eggs, the remaining ½ cup sour cream, and the ½ cup oil; beat with an electric mixer on low for 30 seconds. Scrape down the side of bowl; beat on medium for 2 minutes more. Pour enough of the batter into prepared bowl to fill half full. Pour the remaining batter into prepared muffin cups, filling each two-thirds full.

5. Bake cupcakes for 14 to 18 minutes or until a toothpick inserted in centers comes out clean. Bake batter in bowl for 45 to 55 minutes or until a toothpick inserted in center comes out clean. Cool cupcakes completely on a wire rack. Cool cake in bowl on a wire rack for 15 minutes; carefully remove from bowl. Cool completely on wire rack.

6. To assemble, place one yellow cake layer on a serving plate. Spread with ½ cup of the chocolate frosting; top with the second yellow cake layer. Spread with ¼ cup of the chocolate frosting. Place chocolate bowl cake on the cake layers. Frost side of the yellow cake layers with buttercream frosting, using upward strokes to resemble a cupcake wrapper. Frost chocolate cake top and cupcakes with the remaining chocolate frosting. Decorate cupcake cake with jelly beans and sprinkle cupcakes with confetti sprinkles.

Pineapple Pound Cake

Prep 20 minutes   **Bake** 45 minutes   **Cool** 35 minutes   **Oven** 350°F   **Makes** 8 servings

	Nonstick cooking spray
1	**can (20 ounces) pineapple slices,** *Dole*®
1	**package (16 ounces) pound cake mix,** *Betty Crocker*®
¾	**cup unsweetened pineapple juice,** *Dole*®
2	**eggs**
½	**cup packed brown sugar,** *Domino*®/*C&H*®
2	**tablespoons butter**

1. Preheat oven to 350°F. Spray a 9×5-inch loaf pan with cooking spray; set aside.

2. Drain pineapple, reserving juice. Set aside 3 of the pineapple slices and the reserved juice. Finely chop the remaining pineapple slices; set aside.

3. In a large mixing bowl, combine cake mix, the ¾ cup pineapple juice, and the eggs; beat with an electric mixer on low for 30 seconds. Scrape down the side of bowl; beat on medium for 3 minutes more. Stir in chopped pineapple. Pour into prepared loaf pan.

4. Bake for 45 to 50 minutes or until a toothpick inserted near center comes out clean. Cool in pan on a wire rack for 15 minutes; carefully remove from pan. Cool completely on wire rack.

5. Add enough water to the reserved pineapple juice to make ⅔ cup liquid total. In a small skillet, combine water-juice mixture and brown sugar. Cook over medium-high heat until nearly boiling. Add the reserved 3 pineapple slices; cook about 4 minutes or until sauce thickens slightly. Remove from heat; stir in butter until melted.

6. To serve, place pound cake on a serving plate. Arrange pineapple slices on top; pour sugar mixture over cake.

Pineapple
Pound cake
$400

Cream Marzipan Cake

Prep 25 minutes   **Bake** 45 minutes   **Cool** 35 minutes   **Stand** 30 minutes   **Oven** 350°F   **Makes** 10 servings

CAKE

Nonstick cooking spray

1   tube (7 ounces) marzipan, *Odense*®

½   cup (1 stick) butter, softened

4   eggs

1   package (18.25 ounces) French vanilla cake mix, *Duncan Hines*®

1¼   cups cream soda, *IBC*®

FROSTING

⅓   cup butter

½   cup packed dark brown sugar, *Domino*®/*C&H*®

     Pinch salt

¼   cup milk

1   teaspoon brandy extract, *McCormick*®

1½   cups powdered sugar, sifted, *Domino*®/*C&H*®

1. Preheat oven to 350°F. Spray a 9×3-inch round cake pan or springform pan with cooking spray; set aside.

2. In a large microwave-safe mixing bowl, microwave marzipan on high for 1 to 2 minutes or until softened. (If any hard pieces remain, grate them into bowl.) Add the ½ cup butter and the eggs; beat with an electric mixer on low for 30 seconds. Scrape down the side of bowl; add cake mix and cream soda. Beat on medium for 2 minutes more. Pour batter into prepared pan.

3. Bake for 45 to 50 minutes or until a toothpick inserted near center comes out clean. Cool in pan on a wire rack for 10 minutes; remove cake from pan. Cool completely on wire rack.

4. For frosting, in a small saucepan, melt the ⅓ cup butter over medium-high heat. Add brown sugar and salt, stirring until sugar melts. Add milk; bring to boiling. Remove from heat; stir in the brandy extract. Cool mixture for 15 minutes. Add powdered sugar, stirring until combined.

5. Pour frosting over top of cake on rack. Let stand for 30 minutes to allow frosting to harden.

Island Cake

Prep 25 minutes   **Bake** 45 minutes   **Cool** 35 minutes   **Stand** 15 minutes   **Oven** 350°F   **Makes** 12 servings

Nonstick cooking spray

¼   **cup sweetened shredded coconut, toasted,** *Baker's*®

¼   **cup nut topping,** *Diamond of California*®

1   **package (18.25 ounces) butter-recipe yellow cake mix,** *Duncan Hines*®

1   **package (4-serving-size) instant coconut cream pudding and pie filling mix,** *Jell-O*®

1¼   **cups (2½ sticks) butter, softened**

1   **cup cream soda**

½   **cup milk**

4   **eggs**

1   **cup powdered sugar, sifted,** *Domino*®/*C&H*®

¼   **cup water**

1. Preheat oven to 350°F. Spray a 10-inch fluted tube pan with cooking spray. Sprinkle toasted coconut and nut topping on the bottom of the pan; set aside.

2. In a large mixing bowl, combine cake mix and pudding mix. Add ½ cup of the butter, ½ cup of the cream soda, the milk, and eggs. Beat with an electric mixer on low for 30 seconds. Scrape down the side of bowl; beat on medium for 2 minutes more. Pour batter into prepared pan.

3. Bake for 45 to 50 minutes or until a toothpick inserted in center of cake comes out clean. Cool in pan on a wire rack for 15 minutes; remove from pan. Cool completely on wire rack.

4. For glaze, in a small saucepan, melt the remaining ¾ cup butter over medium-high heat. Stir in powdered sugar and the water. Bring to boiling; cook and stir for 2 to 3 minutes or until slightly thickened. Remove from heat; stir in the remaining ½ cup cream soda.

5. To serve, place cake on a serving plate. Using a wooden skewer, poke holes all over top of cake. Pour half the glaze over hole-studded top; let stand for 15 minutes. Pour remaining glaze over cake.

Chocolate Chip Cake
with Cherry Syrup

Prep 20 minutes   **Bake** 35 minutes   **Cool** 35 minutes   **Oven** 350°F   **Makes** 8 servings

Nonstick cooking spray

1   pouch (17.5 ounces) double chocolate chunk cookie mix, *Betty Crocker*®

1   cup baking mix, *Bisquick*®

¼   cup unsweetened cocoa powder, *Hershey's*®

1   cup chocolate milk, *Nesquik*®

2   tablespoons vegetable oil

1   cup frozen cherries, *Dole*®

½   cup cherry preserves, *Tropical*®

2   tablespoons light-color corn syrup, *Karo*®

1. Preheat oven to 350°F. Spray a 9-inch round cake pan with cooking spray; set aside.

2. In a large mixing bowl, combine cookie mix, baking mix, and cocoa powder. Add chocolate milk and oil; beat with an electric mixer on medium for 2 minutes. Pour into prepared pan.

3. Bake for 35 to 40 minutes or until a toothpick inserted near center comes out clean. Cool in pan on a wire rack for 10 minutes; remove from pan. Cool completely on wire rack.

4. In a medium microwave-safe bowl, combine frozen cherries, preserves, and corn syrup; microwave on medium about 4 minutes or until preserves are melted and mixture is heated through. Cut cake into wedges; top each serving with some of the cherry mixture.

Blueberry Lattice Cake

Prep 35 minutes   **Bake** 35 minutes   **Cool** 35 minutes   **Oven** 350°F   **Makes** 12 servings

Nonstick cooking spray

1   package (18.25 ounces) white cake mix, *Duncan Hines*®

1   package (4-serving-size) instant white chocolate pudding mix, *Jell-O*®

1   cup milk

½   cup vegetable oil

3   egg whites

1   can (15 ounces) blueberries in light syrup, drained, *Oregon*®

2   containers (12 ounces each) whipped vanilla frosting, *Duncan Hines*®

¾   cup white baking chips, melted, *Nestlé*®

¾   cup powdered sugar, sifted, *Domino*®/*C&H*®

Fresh blueberries

1. Preheat oven to 350°F. Spray two 9-inch round cake pans with cooking spray; set aside.

2. In a large mixing bowl, combine cake mix and pudding mix. Add milk, oil, and egg whites; beat with an electric mixer on low for 30 seconds. Scrape down the side of bowl; beat on medium for 2 minutes more. Fold in drained blueberries. Pour batter into prepared pans.

3. Bake for 35 to 40 minutes or until a toothpick inserted near centers comes out clean. Cool in pans on a wire rack for 10 minutes; remove from pans. Cool completely on wire rack.

4. For white frosting, in a medium bowl, combine vanilla frosting and melted white baking chips.

5. To assemble, place one cake layer on a serving plate. Spread with ½ cup of the white frosting; top with second cake layer. Set aside 1½ cups of the white frosting. Frost the side and the top of the cake with the remaining white frosting. In a medium bowl, beat powdered sugar and the reserved 1½ cups white frosting on low until combined.

6. To decorate, insert a basketweave decorating tip into a pastry bag; fill with the powdered sugar-frosting mixture. Starting on the far left edge of cake top, pipe a long stripe of icing straight across top of cake. Cover cake top with additional stripes, spaced ¼ inch apart. Turn the cake 45 degrees; pipe additional stripes of icing across the original strips, spaced ¼ inch apart. Pipe a border around top edge of the cake. Garnish cake with fresh blueberries.

Cupcake Craze

Cupcakes have come a long way since they were considered child's play. These whimsical little cakes will bring a smile to everyone no matter their age.

Cappuccino Fudge Cupcakes

Prep 30 minutes   **Stand** 2 hours   **Bake** 13 minutes   **Cool** 30 minutes   **Oven** 350°F   **Makes** 24 cupcakes

¾   cup semisweet chocolate chips, *Nestle*®

½   cup heavy cream

1¼   cups plus 2 tablespoons espresso and cream coffee drink (double shot), *Starbucks*®

1   cup powdered sugar, *Domino*®/*C&H*®

¼   cup plus 6 tablespoons Italian cappuccino coffee drink mix, *General Foods International*®

¼   cup sweetened condensed milk, *Eagle Brand*®

1   package (18.3 ounces) fudge brownie mix, *Duncan Hines*®

1¼   cups self-rising flour

3   eggs

½   cup vegetable oil

1. Place chocolate chips in a medium bowl; set aside. In a small saucepan, heat cream over medium heat until nearly boiling. Pour cream over chocolate chips; stir until smooth.

2. In another medium bowl, stir together 2 tablespoons of the espresso drink, the powdered sugar, 6 tablespoons of the coffee drink mix, and the sweetened condensed milk, stirring until smooth. Set aside ½ cup of the coffee mixture. Stir the remaining coffee mixture into the chocolate mixture. Let stand at room temperature to thicken (about 2 hours).

3. Preheat oven to 350°F. Line twenty-four 2½-inch muffin cups with paper bake cups; set aside.

4. In a large bowl, combine brownie mix, flour, eggs, oil, the remaining 1¼ cups espresso drink, and the remaining ¼ cup coffee drink mix; beat with an electric mixer on medium for 2 minutes. Spoon batter into prepared muffin cups, filling each about two-thirds full.

5. Bake for 13 to 18 minutes or until a toothpick inserted in the centers comes out clean. Cool cupcakes in muffin cups on a wire rack for 5 minutes. Remove cupcakes from muffin cups; cool completely on rack.

6. Frost cupcakes with the thickened chocolate mixture. Spread 1 teaspoon of the reserved coffee mixture on top of each frosted cupcake; swirl mixtures together.

Banana Split Cupcakes

Prep 25 minutes   **Bake** 16 minutes   **Cool** 30 minutes   **Oven** 350°F   **Makes** 24 cupcakes

1   package (18.25 ounces) banana supreme cake mix, *Duncan Hines*®

1⅓   cups banana-pineapple nectar, *Kern's*®

⅓   cup vegetable oil

3   eggs

1   can (8 ounces) crushed pineapple, *Dole*®

1   can (12 ounces) whipped cream frosting, *Betty Crocker*®

2   tablespoons powdered sugar, *Domino*®/*C&H*®

1   teaspoon imitation strawberry extract, *McCormick*®

2   drops red food coloring, *McCormick*®

1   can (12 ounces) whipped vanilla frosting, *Duncan Hines*®

1   can (12 ounces) whipped chocolate frosting, *Duncan Hines*®

½   cup nut topping, *Fisher*®

24   maraschino cherries with stems, drained and patted dry

1. Preheat oven to 350°F. Line twenty-four 2½-inch muffin cups with paper bake cups; set aside.

2. In a large mixing bowl, beat cake mix, nectar, oil, and eggs with an electric mixer on low for 30 seconds. Scrape down side of bowl; beat for 2 minutes on medium. Add crushed pineapple; stir until combined. Spoon batter into prepared muffin cups, filling each about two-thirds full.

3. Bake for 16 to 20 minutes or until a toothpick inserted in the centers comes out clean. Cool cupcakes in muffin cups on a wire rack for 5 minutes. Remove cupcakes from muffin cups; cool completely on rack.

4. For the strawberry frosting, in a medium bowl, stir together whipped cream frosting, powdered sugar, strawberry extract, and red food coloring until smooth.

5. To frost cupcakes, insert a large round tip into a large pastry bag. Fill pastry bag half full with equal amounts of the strawberry, vanilla, and chocolate frostings, placing each frosting in a wide strip along the side of the bag (you'll have 3 separate strips of frosting). Pipe a large swirl of frosting on each cupcake, refilling pastry bag with frostings as needed. Sprinkle 1 teaspoon of the nut topping on each cupcake; top each cupcake with a maraschino cherry.

Beehive Cupcakes

Prep 40 minutes   **Bake** 15 minutes   **Cool** 30 minutes   **Stand** 30 minutes   **Oven** 350°F   **Makes** 24 cupcakes

I	package (18.25 ounces) butter-recipe yellow cake mix, *Betty Crocker*®
1½	cups (3 sticks) butter, softened
¾	cup water
½	cup plus 3 tablespoons honey, *Sue Bee*®
3	eggs
I	cup vegetable shortening, *Crisco*®
8	cups powdered sugar, sifted, *Domino*®/*C&H*®
5	drops yellow food coloring, *McCormick*®
¼	cup heavy cream
I	tube (4.25 ounces) yellow decorating icing, *Cake Mate*®
48	black jelly beans, *Jelly Belly*®
96	sliced almonds, *Planters*®

1. Preheat oven to 350°F. Line twenty-four 2½-inch muffin cups with paper bake cups; set aside.

2. In a large mixing bowl, beat cake mix, ½ cup of the butter, the water, the ½ cup honey, and the eggs with an electric mixer on low for 30 seconds. Scrape down side of bowl; beat for 2 minutes on medium. Spoon batter into prepared muffin cups, filling each about two-thirds full.

3. Bake for 15 to 18 minutes or until a toothpick inserted in the centers comes out clean. Cool cupcakes in muffin cups on a wire rack for 5 minutes. Remove cupcakes from muffin cups; cool completely on rack.

4. For yellow frosting, in a large mixing bowl, beat shortening and the remaining 1 cup butter with electric mixer on medium until fluffy. Add powdered sugar, the remaining 3 tablespoons honey, and the yellow food coloring. Beat until combined. Add cream, 1 tablespoon at a time, and beat on high until desired thickness.

5. To create beehives, insert a large round decorating tip into a large pastry bag. Fill pastry bag with yellow frosting. Pipe a cone of frosting in the center top of each cupcake, starting from the outer edge and working inward and upward to shape a hive.

6. To create bees, pipe yellow decorating icing in thin horizontal lines on black jelly beans. Let icing stand for 30 minutes. Insert 2 striped jelly beans on each frosting hive. For wings, insert an end of a sliced almond on each side of each striped jelly bean.

Maple and Cream Cheese Cupcakes

Prep 20 minutes   **Bake** 16 minutes   **Cool** 30 minutes   **Oven** 350°F   **Makes** 24 cupcakes

1   package (18.25 ounces) vanilla cake mix, *Duncan Hines*®

1   cup evaporated milk, *Carnation*®

1/2   cup pure maple syrup, *Maple Grove Farms of Vermont*®

1/3   cup canola oil

3   eggs

1 1/2 teaspoons imitation maple flavoring, *McCormick*®

1   can (12 ounces) whipped cream cheese frosting, *Duncan Hines*®

1   cup plus 2 tablespoons powdered sugar, sifted, *Domino*®/*C&H*®

1/2   cup coarsely chopped glazed pecans, *Emerald*®

1. Preheat oven to 350°F. Line twenty-four 2 1/2-inch muffin cups with paper bake cups; set aside.

2. In a large mixing bowl, beat cake mix, evaporated milk, 1/4 cup of the maple syrup, the oil, eggs, and maple flavor with an electric mixer on low for 30 seconds. Scrape down side of bowl; beat for 2 minutes on medium. Spoon batter into prepared muffin cups, filling each about two-thirds full.

3. Bake for 16 to 20 minutes or until a toothpick inserted in the centers comes out clean. Cool cupcakes in muffin cups on a wire rack for 5 minutes. Remove cupcakes from muffin cups; cool completely on rack.

4. In a medium bowl, stir together cream cheese frosting, powdered sugar, and the remaining 1/4 cup maple syrup until smooth. Frost cooled cupcakes with maple cream cheese frosting. Sprinkle with chopped glazed pecans.

Root Beer Cupcakes

Prep 30 minutes   **Bake** 18 minutes   **Cool** 30 minutes   **Oven** 350°F   **Makes** 24 cupcakes

1   package (18.25 ounces) devil's
       food cake mix, *Duncan Hines®*

1⅓   cups root beer, *A&W®*

½   cup vegetable oil

3   eggs

1   can (12 ounces) whipped fluffy
       white frosting, *Duncan Hines®*

1   teaspoon root beer concentrate,*
       McCormick®

       **Root beer-flavor candy, crushed
       (optional), *A&W®***

       24 straws (optional)

1. Preheat oven to 350°F. Line twenty-four 2½-inch muffin cups with paper bake cups; set aside.

2. In a large mixing bowl, beat together cake mix, root beer, oil, and eggs with an electric mixer on low for 30 seconds. Scrape down side of bowl; beat for 2 minutes on medium. Spoon batter into prepared muffin cups, filling each about two-thirds full.

3. Bake for 18 to 22 minutes or until a toothpick inserted in the centers comes out clean. Cool cupcakes in muffin cups on a wire rack for 5 minutes. Remove cupcakes from muffin cups; cool completely on rack.

4. In a medium bowl, combine frosting and root beer concentrate; stir until well mixed. Frost each cupcake with root beer frosting. If desired, dip edges of each cupcake in crushed root beer candies. If desired, remove and discard bottom halves of straws. Insert a straw top in each cupcake.

*Note: If you can't find root beer concentrate, substitute French vanilla or vanilla extract.

Heavenly Hash Cupcakes

Prep 20 minutes   **Bake** 18 minutes   **Cool** 45 minutes   **Oven** 350°F   **Makes** 24 cupcakes

1   package (18.25 ounces) butter-recipe yellow cake mix, *Betty Crocker®*

1²⁄₃   cups buttermilk

¹⁄₂   cup (1 stick) butter, softened

3   eggs

2   cans (12 ounces each) whipped chocolate frosting, *Duncan Hines®*

1   cup tiny marshmallows, *Kraft®*

¹⁄₂   cup chopped pecans, *Planters®*

¹⁄₂   cup chopped almonds, *Planters®*

1. Preheat oven to 350°F. Line twenty-four 2¹⁄₂-inch muffin cups with paper bake cups; set aside.

2. In a large mixing bowl, beat cake mix, buttermilk, butter, and eggs with an electric mixer on low for 30 seconds. Scrape down side of bowl; beat for 2 minutes on medium. Spoon batter into prepared muffin cups, filling each about two-thirds full.

3. Bake for 18 to 22 minutes or until a toothpick inserted in the centers comes out clean. Cool cupcakes in muffin cups on a wire rack for 5 minutes. Remove cupcakes from muffin cups; cool completely on rack.

4. Meanwhile, for frosting, in a large microwave-safe bowl, microwave chocolate frosting on high for 30 seconds. Remove from microwave. Stir in marshmallows, pecans, and almonds until well mixed. Cool for 15 minutes. Top each cupcake with about 2¹⁄₂ tablespoons of the frosting. Cool for 30 minutes before serving.

Chocolate Crater Cupcakes

Prep 20 minutes   **Bake** 20 minutes   **Cool** 30 minutes   **Oven** 350°F   **Makes** 30 cupcakes

1   cup sweetened shredded coconut, *Baker's*®

1   cup chopped walnuts, *Planters*®

1   package (19.5 ounces) dark chocolate cake mix, *Duncan Hines*®

1⅓   cups chocolate milk, *Nesquik*®

½   cup vegetable oil

3   eggs

4   ounces cream cheese, softened, *Philadelphia*®

¼   cup (½ stick) butter, softened

1   cup powdered sugar, sifted, *Domino*®/*C&H*®

5   tablespoons miniature semisweet chocolate chips, *Nestlé*®

1. Preheat oven to 350°F. Line thirty 2½-inch muffin cups with paper bake cups; set pans aside.

2. In a small bowl, combine coconut and walnuts. Spoon about 1 tablespoon of the coconut mixture into each baking cup; set aside.

3. In a large mixing bowl, beat cake mix, chocolate milk, oil, and eggs with an electric mixer on low for 30 seconds. Scrape down side of bowl; beat for 2 minutes on medium. Spoon batter into prepared muffin cups, filling each about half full.

4. In a medium mixing bowl, beat cream cheese and butter with an electric mixer on low until well mixed. Add powdered sugar; beat until smooth. Spoon a heaping teaspoon of the cream cheese mixture on the batter in each baking cup. Sprinkle cream cheese mixture in each cup with ½ teaspoon of the miniature chocolate chips.

5. Bake for 20 to 24 minutes or until a toothpick inserted in the centers of the cake part comes out clean. Cool cupcakes in muffin cups on a wire rack for 5 minutes. Remove cupcakes from muffin cups; cool completely on rack.

Chocolate Molten Cupcakes

Prep 30 minutes   **Chill** 2 hours   **Freeze** 1 hour   **Bake** 16 minutes   **Cool** 40 minutes   **Oven** 350°F   **Makes** 24 cupcakes

½   of a 12-ounce package semisweet chocolate chips, *Nestle*®

½   cup heavy cream

1   package (18.25 ounces) German chocolate cake mix, *Duncan Hines*®

1⅓   cups chocolate milk, *Nesquik*®

½   cup vegetable oil

3   eggs

    Powdered sugar, *Domino*®/*C&H*®

1. Place chocolate chips in a medium bowl; set aside. In a small saucepan, heat cream over medium heat until nearly boiling. Pour cream over chocolate chips; stir until smooth. Cover bowl and refrigerate for 2 hours. Line a baking sheet with parchment paper. Using a 1-teaspoon measure, scoop 24 balls from chocolate mixture. Place balls on baking sheet; freeze for 1 hour.

2. Preheat oven to 350°F. Line twenty-four 2½-inch muffin cups with paper bake cups; set aside.

3. In a large bowl, beat cake mix, chocolate milk, oil, and eggs with an electric mixer on low for 30 seconds. Scrape down side of the bowl; beat for 2 minutes on medium. Spoon batter into prepared muffin cups, filling each about half full. Place a frozen chocolate ball on batter in each muffin cup. Spoon more batter over each chocolate ball, filling each muffin cup about three-fourths full. (Do not push ball down into batter.)

4. Bake for 16 to 20 minutes or until a toothpick inserted in the cupcakes comes out clean. Cool cupcakes in muffin cups on a wire rack for 5 minutes. Remove cupcakes from muffin cups; cool completely on rack.

5. Just before serving, sift powdered sugar over cupcakes.*

*Note: If you prefer, omit the powdered sugar and frost the cupcakes with 1 can (12 ounces) whipped chocolate frosting, *Duncan Hines*®.

Chocolate-Chocolate Cherry Cupcakes

Prep 30 minutes   **Bake** 12 minutes   **Cool** 30 minutes   **Stand** 10 minutes   **Oven** 350°F   **Makes** 24 cupcakes

1   package (18.25 ounces) butter-recipe chocolate cake mix, *Betty Crocker*®

1⅓   cups cranberry-cherry juice, *Ocean Spray*®

½   cup (1 stick) butter, softened

3   eggs

½   cup cherry pie filling, *Comstock*® or *Wilderness*®

1¼   cups white baking chips, *Nestlé*®

7   tablespoons heavy cream

2½   teaspoons light-color corn syrup, *Karo*®

1¼   cups whipped fluffy white frosting, *Duncan Hines*®

⅓   cup semisweet chocolate chips, *Nestlé*®

1   jar (10 ounces) maraschino cherries with stems, drained

1. Preheat oven to 350°F. Line twenty-four 2½-inch muffin cups with paper bake cups; set aside.

2. In a large mixing bowl, beat cake mix, cranberry-cherry juice, butter, and eggs with an electric mixer on low for 30 seconds. Scrape down side of bowl; beat for 2 minutes on medium. Spoon 2 tablespoons of the batter into each prepared muffin cup. Spoon 1 teaspoon of the cherry pie filling on batter in each cup; top with another 1 tablespoon of the batter.

3. Bake for 12 to 16 minutes or until a toothpick inserted in the cupcakes comes out clean. Cool cupcakes in muffin cups on a wire rack for 5 minutes. Remove cupcakes from muffin cups; cool completely on rack.

4. For white frosting, place white baking chips in a medium bowl; set aside. In a small saucepan, heat cream and corn syrup over medium heat until nearly boiling. Pour over white baking chips; stir until completely smooth. Let stand for 10 minutes. Stir cream mixture into white frosting until well mixed; set aside.

5. In a small microwave-safe bowl, microwave semisweet chocolate chips on medium for 2 minutes, stirring every 30 seconds. Place maraschino cherries on paper towels to dry. Dip each dry cherry into melted semisweet chocolate; place on waxed paper-lined baking sheet until chocolate hardens.

6. Frost each cupcake with white chocolate frosting; top with a chocolate-covered cherry.

Cookies, Cookies

Whether it's a half dozen or a baker's dozen, cookies are always a big hit at bake sales. Fill the cookie jar, serve them as dessert, or package them prettily as gifts.

Chocolate Mint Chip Cookies

Prep 25 minutes   **Bake** 14 minutes per batch   **Cool** 5 minutes per batch   **Oven** 350°F   **Makes** 22 cookies

1	package (19.9 ounces) dark chocolate brownie mix, *Duncan Hines*®
½	cup self-rising flour
⅓	cup vegetable oil
¼	cup chocolate milk, *Nesquik*®
1	egg
1½	teaspoons mint extract, *McCormick*®
20	crème de menthe thins, unwrapped and chopped, *Andes*®
1¾	cups powdered sugar, sifted, *Domino*®/*C&H*®
3	tablespoons water
1	teaspoon meringue powder,* *Wilton*®

1. Preheat oven to 350°F. Line cookie sheet(s) with parchment paper; set aside.

2. In a large mixing bowl, combine brownie mix and self-rising flour. Add oil, chocolate milk, egg, and 1 teaspoon of the mint extract, stirring until combined. Gently stir in crème de menthe thins. Drop dough by heaping tablespoonfuls (or use a 2-tablespoon scoop) onto prepared cookie sheet(s), spacing cookies 2 inches apart.

3. Bake for 14 to 16 minutes or until set in centers. Cool on cookie sheet(s) for 5 minutes. Transfer cookies to a wire rack; cool completely.

4. For mint glaze, in a medium bowl, stir together powdered sugar, the water, meringue powder, and the remaining ½ teaspoon mint extract, stirring until a glaze consistency. Stir in more water if necessary.

5. Roll the edges of the cooled cookies in the mint glaze. Lay cookies flat on a wire cooling rack and let stand until glaze hardens.

*Note: Meringue powder is available at cake decorating stores, crafts stores, or online at wilton.com.

Banana-Cashew Cookies

Prep 15 minutes   **Bake** 13 minutes per patch   **Cool** 5 minutes per batch   **Oven** 350°F   **Makes** 22 cookies

1   package (17.1 ounces) banana nut muffin mix, *Krusteaz*®

⅓   cup granulated sugar, *Domino*®/*C&H*®

⅓   cup packed brown sugar, *Domino*®/*C&H*®

½   cup banana milk,* *Nesquik*®*

¼   cup (½ stick) butter, softened

2   eggs

1½   cups chopped cashews, *Planters*®

1. Preheat oven to 350°F. Line cookie sheet(s) with parchment paper; set aside.

2. In a large bowl, stir together muffin mix, granulated sugar, and brown sugar. Add banana milk, butter, and eggs, stirring until combined. Gently stir in cashews. Drop dough by heaping tablespoonfuls (or use a 2-tablespoon scoop) onto prepared cookie sheet(s), spacing cookies 2 inches apart.

3. Bake for 13 to 18 minutes or until lightly browned. Cool on cookie sheet(s) for 5 minutes. Transfer cookies to a wire rack; cool completely.

*Note: If you can't find banana milk, use 1 cup regular milk combined with 1 teaspoon imitation banana extract, *McCormick*®.

Butterscotch Chip Cookies

Prep 20 minutes   **Bake** 10 minutes per batch   **Cool** 5 minutes per batch   **Oven** 375°F   **Makes** 27 cookies

1   package (18.25 ounces) yellow cake mix, *Duncan Hines*®

½   cup packed brown sugar, *Domino*®/*C&H*®

5   tablespoons buttermilk

¼   cup (½ stick) butter, melted

1   egg

1   cup butterscotch chips, *Nestlé*®

1   cup chopped pecans, *Planters*®

1. Preheat oven to 375°F. Line cookie sheet(s) with parchment paper; set aside.

2. In a large bowl, combine cake mix and brown sugar. Add buttermilk, butter, and egg, stirring until well mixed. Add butterscotch chips and pecans, stirring until combined. Drop dough by heaping tablespoonfuls (or use a 2-tablespoon scoop) onto prepared cookie sheet(s), spacing cookies 2 inches apart.

3. Bake for 10 to 13 minutes or until set in centers. Cool on cookie sheet(s) for 5 minutes. Transfer cookies to a wire rack; cool completely.

Crunchy Cocoa-Coconut Cookies

Prep 15 minutes   **Bake** 13 minutes per batch   **Cool** 5 minutes per batch   **Oven** 350°F   **Makes** 24 cookies

1   pouch (17.5 ounces) double chocolate chunk cookie mix, *Betty Crocker*®

1   teaspoon ground cinnamon, *McCormick*®

¼   cup vegetable oil

1   egg

2   tablespoons chocolate milk, *Nesquik*®

1¼   cups chocolate-flavored crisp rice cereal, *Cocoa Pebbles*®

¾   cup sweetened shredded coconut, *Baker's*®

1. Preheat oven to 350°F. Line cookie sheet(s) with parchment paper; set aside.

2. In a large bowl, combine cookie mix and cinnamon. Add oil, egg, and chocolate milk, stirring until well mixed. Gently stir in cereal and coconut. Drop dough by heaping tablespoonfuls (or use a 2-tablespoon scoop) onto prepared cookie sheet(s), spacing cookies 2 inches apart.

3. Bake for 13 to 15 minutes or until set in centers. Cool on cookie sheet(s) for 5 minutes. Transfer cookies to a wire rack; cool completely.

Minty Thins

Prep 15 minutes   **Stand** 2 hours   **Makes** 18 cookies

1   tablespoon plus 1 teaspoon vegetable shortening, *Crisco*®

2   teaspoons mint extract, *McCormick*®

1   cup semisweet chocolate chips, *Nestlé*®

18   chocolate wafer cookies, *Nabisco*® *Famous*
       Green sparkling sugar, *India Tree*®

1. In a medium microwave-safe bowl, combine shortening and mint extract; microwave on high for 30 seconds. Add chocolate chips; microwave on medium for 1½ minutes, stirring every 30 seconds. Stir chocolate mixture until smooth.

2. Dip bottom of each wafer cookie into chocolate mixture; spread smooth with a knife. Place cookies, chocolate-covered sides up, on a wire rack. Let stand about 1 hour or until chocolate hardens.

3. Repeat with other side of each wafer cookie so whole cookie is covered with chocolate. Let stand until chocolate hardens, sprinkling with sparkling sugar before chocolate hardens.

Note: These cookies freeze well. Place cookies in a single layer in an air-tight freezer container. Freeze up to 1 month.

Lemonade Creams

Prep 35 minutes   **Chill** 2 hours   **Bake** 9 minutes per batch   **Cool** 5 minutes per batch   **Oven** 375°F   **Makes** 44 cookies

1   pouch (17.5 ounces) sugar cookie mix, *Betty Crocker®*

¼   cup cook-and-serve lemon pudding and pie filling mix, *Jell-O®*

2   tablespoons all-purpose flour

⅓   cup cold butter, cut into pieces

10   to 12 tablespoons frozen lemonade concentrate, thawed, *Minute Maid®*

3   teaspoons vegetable shortening, *Crisco®*

3   drops yellow food coloring, *McCormick®*

2¼   cups powdered sugar, *Domino®/C&H®*

1. In a large bowl, whisk together cookie mix, dry lemon pudding mix, and flour. Add butter pieces and 4 to 6 tablespoons of the lemonade concentrate, 1 tablespoon at a time, using your hands to work mixture into a dough. On a lightly floured surface, shape dough in an 11-inch log. Wrap log in plastic wrap. Chill in refrigerator for at least 2 hours.

2. Preheat oven to 375°F. Line cookie sheet(s) with parchment paper; set aside.

3. Remove dough from refrigerator. Slice log in ¼-inch slices. Shape slices in circles; place dough circles on prepared cookie sheet(s), spacing circles 2 inches apart.

4. Bake for 9 to 11 minutes or just until starting to brown. Cool on cookie sheet(s) for 5 minutes. Transfer cookies to a wire rack; cool completely.

5. For lemon glaze, in a large microwave-safe bowl, combine shortening and food coloring. Microwave on high for 30 seconds. Sift powdered sugar into shortening mixture, stirring until well mixed. Stir in enough of the remaining lemonade concentrate, about 6 tablespoons, to make a thick glaze.

6. Dip bottoms of cooled cookies into lemon glaze. Lay cookies upside down on wire rack; let stand until glaze hardens.

PB Caramel Sandwich Cookie Bites

Prep 30 minutes   **Bake** 5 minutes per batch   **Cool** 5 minutes per batch
Oven 350°F   **Makes** 22 cookie sandwiches

COOKIES

1	pouch (17.5 ounces) peanut butter cookie mix, *Betty Crocker®*
3	tablespoons cake flour, *Swans Down®*
3	tablespoons vegetable oil
1	egg
1	tablespoon milk
11	individually wrapped caramels, unwrapped and cut in half, *Kraft®*

FILLING

1/3	cup creamy peanut butter, *Skippy® Natural*
3	tablespoons caramel topping, *Smucker's®*

1. For cookies, preheat oven to 350°F. Line cookie sheet(s) with parchment paper; set aside.

2. In a large bowl, combine cookie mix and cake flour. Add oil, egg, and milk; stir until dough comes together. Scoop 1 tablespoon of the dough; use your hands to shape into a ball. Repeat to make 44 balls total. Arrange half the dough balls on prepared cookie sheet(s), spacing balls 1½ inches apart. Gently press a caramel half into the center of each dough ball on cookie sheet(s). Bake for 5 to 7 minutes or until edges are lightly browned. Cool on cookie sheet(s) for 5 minutes. Transfer cookies to a wire rack; cool completely.

3. Arrange remaining dough balls on cookie sheet(s), spacing balls 1½ inches apart. Using your fingertips, gently flatten each ball. Bake for 5 to 7 minutes or until edges are lightly browned. Cool on cookie sheet(s) for 5 minutes. Transfer cookies to a wire rack; cool completely.

4. For filling, in a small bowl, stir together peanut butter and caramel topping until well mixed.

5. To make sandwich cookies, spoon a heaping teaspoonful of the filling onto each plain cookie. Top with caramel cookies.

Butter Toffee Flower Sandwiches

Prep 35 minutes   **Chill** 30 minutes   **Bake** 8 minutes per batch
Cool 5 minutes per batch   **Oven** 375°F   **Makes** 12 cookie sandwiches

COOKIES

1	pouch (17.5 ounces) chocolate chip cookie mix, *Betty Crocker*®
¾	cup all-purpose flour
¼	cup vegetable oil
2	eggs
1	teaspoon imitation butter flavoring, *McCormick*®

FILLING

1	cup whipped buttercream frosting, *Betty Crocker*®
¼	cup powdered sugar, sifted, *Domino*®/*C&H*®
¾	cup toffee bits, *Heath*®

1. Spoon cookie mix into a wire-mesh strainer set over a large bowl. Sift cookie mix through strainer, leaving chocolate chips in strainer (reserve chocolate chips for another use). Add flour, oil, eggs, and butter flavoring to cookie mix in bowl; stir until dough comes together. Shape into a ball; wrap in plastic wrap. Chill dough in refrigerator for at least 30 minutes.

2. Meanwhile, preheat oven to 375°F. Line cookie sheet(s) with parchment paper; set aside.

3. On a lightly floured surface, roll out chilled dough to ¼-inch thickness. Using a 3-inch flower cookie cutter, cut 12 shapes from dough. Using a 1-inch round cookie cutter, cut out each flower center. Reroll scrap dough; cut out another 12 flower shapes, but do not cut out centers. Transfer flowers to prepared cookie sheet(s), spacing cookies 2 inches apart.

4. Bake for 8 to 10 minutes or just until starting to brown. Cool on cookie sheet(s) for 5 minutes. Transfer cookies to a wire rack; cool completely.

5. For filling, in a medium bowl, stir together frosting and powdered sugar until well mixed. Gently stir in ½ cup of the toffee bits.

6. Spoon a heaping tablespoon of the filling onto each of the whole flower cookies. Top each with a cutout flower cookie. Sprinkle a scant teaspoon of the remaining toffee bits in the center of each cutout.

Toasted Coconut Gooey Goodies

Prep 20 minutes   **Bake** 15 minutes   **Oven** 350°F   **Makes** 14 cookies

1¼   cups sweetened shredded coconut, *Baker's*®

24   individual chewy caramels, unwrapped, *Werther's® Original*®

1   tablespoon heavy cream

14   striped shortbread cookies, *Mother's Cookies*®

½   cup semisweet chocolate chips, *Nestlé*®

1. Preheat oven to 350°F. Place a wire rack over a cookie sheet; set aside.

2. Spread coconut on another cookie sheet. Toast for 15 to 20 minutes or until golden brown, stirring with a fork every 5 minutes. Cool completely. Place cooled coconut in a food processor; pulse for a few seconds. Set aside.

3. In a medium microwave-safe bowl, combine caramels and cream; microwave on high about 1 minute or until melted. Gently stir in coconut.

4. Spoon coconut caramel mixture over top of striped shortbread cookies, leaving a hole in the middle. Place cookies on prepared wire rack; cool completely. (Reheat caramel mixture if it hardens.)

5. Place chocolate chips in a small microwave-safe bowl; microwave on medium 1 minute or until melted, stirring every 30 seconds. Place melted chocolate in a disposable piping bag; snip a small piece off end of bag. Pipe 4 lines of chocolate across each cookie. Let stand until chocolate hardens.

PB and Chocolate Chewies

Prep 30 minutes   **Stand** 2 hours   **Makes** 9 cookies

1½   cups plus 2 tablespoons semisweet chocolate chips, *Nestlé*®

½   teaspoon vegetable shortening, *Crisco*®

1   package (5.3 ounces) shortbread rounds, *Walkers*®

¾   cup creamy peanut butter, *Skippy® Natural*

¼   teaspoon vanilla extract, *McCormick*®
     Pinch salt

6   tablespoons powdered sugar, sifted, *Domino®/C&H*®

1. In a small microwave-safe bowl, combine chocolate chips and shortening; microwave on medium 2 minutes or until melted, stirring every 30 seconds.

2. Dip bottom of each shortbread round into chocolate mixture; spread smooth with a knife. Place shortbread rounds, chocolate-covered sides up, on a wire rack. Let stand about 1 hour or until chocolate hardens.

3. Meanwhile, in a medium bowl, beat peanut butter, vanilla extract, and salt with an electric mixer on low until well mixed. Beat in powdered sugar.

4. Turn over shortbread rounds on cooling rack. Spoon 1 tablespoon of the peanut butter mixture into middle of each round. Reheat remaining chocolate mixture in microwave on medium until smooth, stirring often. Spoon chocolate mixture over peanut butter mixture; spread to coat so each cookie is covered with chocolate. Let stand until chocolate hardens.

Stained Glass Cookies

Prep 30 minutes   **Chill** 30 minutes   **Bake** 9 minutes per batch   **Cool** 5 minutes per batch   **Oven** 375°F   **Makes** 12 cookies

Nonstick cooking spray

1   pouch (17.5 ounces) sugar cookie mix, *Betty Crocker®*

3   tablespoons cake flour, *Swans Down®*

1/3   cup cream cheese, softened, *Philadelpia®*

1   egg

1   teaspoon lemon extract, *McCormick®*

8   ounces hard candies (in assorted colors), *Jolly Rancher®* or *Life Savers®*

1. Line cookie sheet(s) with foil; spray with cooking spray and set aside. In a large bowl, combine cookie mix and cake flour. Add cream cheese, egg, and lemon extract, stirring until dough forms. Divide dough in half; shape each half in a ball and flatten to make a disk.

2. On a lightly floured surface, roll out one-half of the dough until 1/4-inch thickness. Using large cookie cutters, cut out shapes. Place cookies on prepared cookie sheet(s), spacing cookies 2 inches apart. Using tiny cookie cutters, cut small shapes from the center of each cookie on cookie sheet(s). Reroll dough scraps and cut out more cookies until all of the dough is used. Chill in refrigerator for at least 30 minutes.

3. Meanwhile, preheat oven to 375°F. Place unwrapped hard candies, sorted by color, in separate zip-top plastic bags. Squeeze air from bags and seal; use a rolling pin to crush candies. Set aside.

4. Remove cookies from refrigerator; fill cutout centers of the cookies with crushed hard candies.

5. Bake for 9 to 12 minutes or just until edges start to turn golden. Cool on cookie sheet(s) for 5 minutes. Transfer cookies to a wire rack; cool completely.

Note: To store cookies, layer between sheets of waxed paper in an airtight container. Cover; seal. Store at room temperature up to 1 week.

Bars & Brownies

A square of something sweet to eat with coffee, tea, or milk is always a welcome treat. Bars and brownies are much loved because they're so easy on busy bakers.

25¢

Chocolate Hazelnut Brownies

Prep 25 minutes   **Bake** 35 minutes   **Cool** 1 hour   **Oven** 350°F   **Makes** 12 servings

Nonstick cooking spray

1   package (18.25 ounces) butter-recipe chocolate cake mix, *Betty Crocker*®

¼   cup brown sugar, *Domino*®/*C&H*®

1¼   cups chocolate hazelnut spread, *Nutella*®

½   cup (1 stick) butter, melted

2   eggs

1   package (2.25 ounces) chopped hazelnuts, *Diamond of California*®

¾   cup powdered sugar, *Domino*®/*C&H*®

¼   cup heavy cream

1. Preheat oven to 350°F. Spray a 9-inch square baking pan with cooking spray; set aside.

2. In a large bowl, stir together cake mix and brown sugar. Add ½ cup of the chocolate hazelnut spread, the melted butter, and eggs; stir until combined (batter will be thick). Stir in hazelnuts. Pour into prepared baking pan.

3. Bake for 35 to 40 minutes or until a toothpick inserted in center comes out clean. Cool in pan on a wire rack.

4. In a medium mixing bowl, beat the remaining ¾ cup chocolate hazelnut spread, the powdered sugar, and cream with an electric mixer on medium until smooth. Spread on cooled brownies.

Banana Walnut Brownies

Prep 30 minutes   **Bake** 30 minutes   **Oven** 350°F   **Makes** 12 brownies

Nonstick cooking spray

1   package (18.25 ounces) chocolate fudge cake mix, *Duncan Hines*®

1   package (4-serving-size) instant banana cream pudding and pie filling mix, *Jell-O*®

⅓   cup brown sugar, *Domino*®/*C&H*®

½   cup vegetable oil

¼   cup chocolate milk, *Nesquik*®

2   eggs

¾   cup finely chopped glazed walnuts, *Emerald*®

1   small banana, cut into 12 slices

12   glazed walnuts, *Emerald*®

1. Preheat oven to 350°F. Spray a 9×13-inch baking pan with cooking spray.

2. In a large bowl, stir together cake mix, pudding mix, and brown sugar. Add oil, chocolate milk, and eggs; stir. Stir in walnuts. Pour into baking pan. Lightly press the 12 banana slices into batter, evenly placing 3 slices crosswise and 4 slices lengthwise. Using a small spatula, smooth batter over banana slices to fully cover. Press 12 glazed walnuts on top of batter, in approximately the same place bananas are covered.

3. Bake for 30 to 35 minutes or until a toothpick inserted in center comes out clean. Cool in pan on a wire rack. Cut brownies so each serving has a glazed walnut on top.

Peanut Butter Cookie Brownie Bars

Prep 20 minutes   **Bake** 50 minutes   **Oven** 350°F   **Makes** 12 servings

Nonstick cooking spray

1   package (19.9 ounces) dark
    chocolate brownie mix,
    Duncan Hines®

½   cup vegetable oil

¼   cup milk

2   eggs

1   package (16 ounces) refrigerated
    filled peanut butter cookie dough,
    Nestlé® Ultimates™

1   package (2.25 ounces) nut
    topping, *Diamond of California*®

1. Preheat oven to 350°F. Spray a 9-inch square baking pan with cooking spray; set aside.

2. In a large bowl, stir together brownie mix, oil, milk, and eggs until well mixed. Pour half the batter into prepared baking pan. Break apart cookie dough pieces; randomly drop pieces on batter. Pour the remaining batter over cookie dough, spreading smoothly. Sprinkle nut topping over top.

3. Bake for 50 to 55 minutes or until a toothpick inserted in center comes out clean. Cool in pan on a wire rack.

Cheesecake Brownies

Prep 20 minutes   **Bake** 40 minutes   **Oven** 350°F   **Makes** 12 brownies

Nonstick cooking spray

1   (7-inch) purchased cheesecake with fruit topping, thawed if
    frozen*

1   package (19.9 ounces) dark chocolate brownie mix,
    Duncan Hines®

2   eggs

½   cup vegetable oil

1. Preheat oven to 350°F. Spray a 9×13-inch baking pan with cooking spray; set aside.

2. Cut cheesecake in bite-size pieces.

3. In a large bowl, stir together brownie mix, eggs, and oil until well mixed (batter will be thick). Gently stir in cheesecake pieces. Spread into prepared baking pan.

4. Bake for 40 to 45 minutes or until brownies are set in center. Cool in pan on a wire rack.

*Note: The cheesecake works best when it is cold, but not frozen.

Chocolate Pudding Bars

Prep 30 minutes   **Bake** 15 minutes   **Cool** 1 hour   **Chill** 2 hours   **Oven** 375°F   **Makes** 16 servings

1   package (12 ounces) semisweet chocolate chips, *Nestle*®

¾   cup heavy cream

     Nonstick cooking spray

1   package (18.25 ounces) butter-recipe chocolate cake mix, *Betty Crocker*®

2   eggs

½   cup (1 stick) butter, melted

2   cups cold chocolate milk, *Nesquik*®

1   package (5.9-ounce) instant chocolate fudge pudding and pie filling mix, *Jell-O*®

1. Place chocolate chips in a medium bowl; set aside. In a small saucepan, heat cream over medium heat until nearly boiling. Pour hot cream over chocolate chips; stir until smooth. Set aside to cool and thicken.

2. Preheat oven to 375°F. Spray a 9×13-inch baking pan with cooking spray; set aside.

3. In a large bowl, combine cake mix, eggs, and melted butter; stir until well mixed. Spread in prepared baking pan.

4. Bake about 15 minutes or until toothpick inserted in center comes out with a few sticky crumbs on it. Cool in pan on a wire rack.

5. In a large bowl, combine chocolate milk and pudding mix; whisk together for 2 minutes. Let stand about 3 minutes or until thickened.

6. Spread an even layer of the pudding mixture over the cooled cake. Top with an even layer of the thickened chocolate mixture.

7. Chill about 2 hours or until top sets. Cut into bars and serve chilled or at room temperature.

Maple Bars

Prep 35 minutes **Cool** 15 minutes + 2 hours **Bake** 30 minutes **Oven** 350°F **Makes** 24 small bars

¼ cup (½ stick) butter

1¼ cups pure maple syrup, *Spring Tree®*

2 tablespoons heavy cream

1 cup powdered sugar, sifted, *Domino®/C&H®*

Nonstick cooking spray

¾ cup quick-cooking rolled oats, *Quaker®*

1 package (16 ounces) pound cake mix, *Betty Crocker®*

1 egg

¾ cup chopped pecans, toasted, *Emerald®*

1. In a small saucepan, melt butter over medium-high heat. Stir in ½ cup of the syrup; cook about 5 minutes or until thickened. Stir in cream; return to boiling. Remove from heat; transfer to a large mixing bowl. Cool for 15 minutes. Gradually add powdered sugar, beating with an electric mixer on low to medium until thickened. Let stand at room temperature about 2 hours or until a spreadable consistency.

2. Preheat oven to 350°F. Spray a 9-inch square baking pan with cooking spray; set aside.

3. Place oats in a food processor or blender; cover and process or blend until finely ground. Pour into a large mixing bowl. Add cake mix, egg, and the remaining ¾ cup syrup. Beat with an electric mixer on low for 1 minute. Spread into prepared baking pan.

4. Bake for 30 to 35 minutes or until a toothpick inserted in center comes out clean. Cool in pan on a wire rack.

5. Spread thickened maple mixture over cooled cake. Sprinkle toasted pecans over top. Cut into bars.

PB&J Chocolate Cream Cheese Bars

Prep 20 minutes **Bake** 15 minutes **Cool** 5 minutes + 1 hour **Chill** 2 hours **Oven** 375°F **Makes** 12 bars

Nonstick cooking spray

1 pouch (17.5 ounces) sugar cookie mix, *Betty Crocker®*

½ cup (1 stick) butter, melted

1 cup peanut butter, *Jif®*

1 container (24 ounces) ready-to-eat cheesecake filling, *Philadelphia® Heavenly Classic*

3 ounces semisweet chocolate, melted and cooled, *Nestlé®*

1 cup strawberry preserves, *Smucker's®*

1. Preheat oven to 375°F. Spray a 9×13-inch baking pan with cooking spray; set aside.

2. In a medium bowl, stir together cookie mix and melted butter until combined. Press into bottom of prepared baking pan.

3. Bake for 15 to 20 minutes or until set in center. Cool in pan on a wire rack for 5 minutes. Spread peanut butter evenly over warm cookie layer. Cool completely.

4. In a medium bowl, stir together cheesecake filling and melted chocolate. Spread chocolate cheesecake mixture evenly over peanut butter. Top with strawberry preserves, spreading evenly. Chill in refrigerator for at least 2 hours.

5. Cut into bars. Store in refrigerator.

Pistachio Cream Bars

Prep 30 minutes   **Bake** 20 minutes   **Cool** 1 hour   **Oven** 375°F   **Makes** 12 bars

1   package (4-serving-size) instant pistachio pudding and pie filling mix, *Jell-O*®

1   can (12 ounces) whipped whipped cream frosting, *Betty Crocker*®

     Nonstick cooking spray

1   package (18.25 ounces) white cake mix, *Duncan Hines*®

½   cup vegetable oil

2   eggs

½   cup finely chopped walnuts or pecans, *Planters*®

½   cup finely chopped dried pineapple, *Sunsweet*®

½   cup sweetened shredded coconut, *Baker's*®

⅓   cup chopped pistachio nuts

1. Add 3 tablespoons of the dry pistachio pudding mix to the whipped cream frosting, stirring until well mixed. Cover and set aside.

2. Preheat oven to 375°F. Spray a 9×13-inch baking pan with cooking spray; set aside.

3. In a large bowl, stir together the remaining dry pistachio pudding mix, the cake mix, oil, and eggs until well mixed. Stir in walnuts, dried pineapple, and coconut until combined. Spread batter into prepared baking pan.

4. Bake for 20 to 25 minutes or until a toothpick inserted in center comes out clean. Cool in pan on a wire rack.

5. Stir frosting mixture; spread over cooled cake. Sprinkle pistachio nuts over top. Cut into bars.

Dark Chocolate Caramel Slices

Prep 20 minutes   **Bake** 10 minutes   **Cool** 10 minutes + 1 hour   **Chill** 1 hour   **Oven** 375°F   **Makes** 16 servings

     Nonstick cooking spray

1   pouch (17.5 ounces) sugar cookie mix, *Betty Crocker*®

½   cup (1 stick) butter, melted

50   individual caramel candies, unwrapped, *Kraft*®

1   tablespoon water

1   cup semisweet chocolate chips, *Nestle*®

1. Preheat oven to 375°F. Spray a 9×13-inch baking pan with cooking spray.

2. In a medium bowl, stir together cookie mix and melted butter until mixture comes together. Press into bottom of prepared baking pan.

3. Bake for 10 to 15 minutes or until set in center. Cool in pan on a wire rack.

4. In a medium saucepan, combine caramels and water over medium-high heat, stirring constantly until smooth. Pour over cookie crust; cool completely.

5. Place chocolate chips in a small microwave-safe bowl; microwave on medium 2 minutes or until melted, stirring every 30 seconds. Spread over caramel layer. Chill in refrigerator about 1 hour or until chocolate hardens.*

***Note:** Remove from refrigerator after 1 hour, before caramel slices become too hard to slice.

Quick Scratch

Perfect for drop-in dinner guests or spur-of-the-moment fundraisers, these speedy treats only look and taste as if they took all day to make.

Apple Dumplings

Prep 30 minutes   **Bake** 20 minutes + 20 minutes   **Cool** 10 minutes   **Oven** 450°F/350°F   **Makes** 4 dumplings

Nonstick cooking spray

¾ cup apple juice, *Tree Top*®

½ cup plus 3 tablespoons packed brown sugar, *Domino*®/*C&H*®

3 tablespoons ginger preserves, *Robertson's*®

3 tablespoons butter

2 teaspoons frozen lemon juice, thawed, *Minute Maid*®

¾ teaspoon pumpkin pie spice, *McCormick*®

3 tablespoons finely chopped mixed dried fruit (such as apricots, cherries, and/or cranberries)

2 tablespoons finely chopped pecans, *Planters*®

1 package (15 ounces) refrigerated pie crusts, *Pillsbury*®

4 Granny Smith apples, peeled and cored

1. Preheat oven to 450°F. Spray a baking sheet with cooking spray; set aside.

2. For the syrup, in a small saucepan, combine apple juice, ½ cup of the brown sugar, the ginger preserves, butter, lemon juice, and ½ teaspoon of the pumpkin pie spice. Bring to boiling over medium-high heat; boil until the liquid is reduced by half or until syrupy consistency. Remove from heat; cool.

3. In a small bowl, toss together the remaining 3 tablespoons brown sugar, the remaining ¼ teaspoon pumpkin pie spice, the dried fruit, and pecans; set aside.

4. On a lightly floured surface, unroll one of the pie crusts; cut in half. Using a rolling pin, roll out each crust half to a 9½-inch-diameter circle. Repeat with the remaining dough to make 4 dough circles.

5. Using a pastry brush, brush a thin layer of the syrup on the peeled apples. Place an apple upside down in the center of 1 of the dough circles. Fill cored apple center with the dried fruit mixture. Pull edges of dough up toward center, covering apple completely; secure top by pressing the dough together. Place, seam side down, on prepared baking sheet; brush the dough with syrup. Repeat to make 4 dumplings.

6. Bake about 20 minutes or until pastry is golden. Remove baking sheet from oven; reduce oven temperature to 350°F. Spoon more of the syrup over dumplings. Bake for 20 to 30 minutes more or until pastry is crisp and apples are tender. Remove from oven; spoon remaining syrup over dumplings. Cool for 10 minutes; serve warm.

Chocolate Fondue

Start to Finish 15 minutes   **Makes** 6 servings

1   cup + 2 tablespoons heavy cream

1   teaspoon instant espresso powder

1   package (12 ounces) milk chocolate chips, *Nestlé®*

2   teaspoons vanilla extract, *McCormick®*

     Dippers*

1. In a medium saucepan, stir together heavy cream and espresso powder. Cook over medium heat until nearly boiling. Add chocolate chips, stirring constantly until chocolate is melted. Stir in vanilla extract.

2. Pour into a fondue pot or a 1½-quart slow cooker to keep warm or transfer to a decorative jar and chill in the refrigerator. Serve with dippers.

*Note: For dippers use
• Purchased brownies or chocolate pound cake, cut in bite-size chunks
• Purchased chocolate muffins or bread, cut in bite-size chunks
• Purchased soft chocolate cookies
• Frozen cheesecake, cut in bite-size chunks

Pear and Cinnamon Charlotte

Prep 20 minutes   **Cook** 10 minutes   **Bake** 30 minutes   **Oven** 400°F   **Makes** 8 servings

16   to 18 slices cinnamon bread, *Cinnabon®*

3   cans (15 ounces each) sliced pears in light syrup, *Del Monte®*

½   cup (1 stick) butter, melted

2   tablespoons packed brown sugar, *Domino®/C&H®*

1   teaspoon frozen lemon juice, thawed, *Minute Maid®*

½   teaspoon pumpkin pie spice, *McCormick®*

¼   cup chopped pecans, *Planters®*

¼   cup apricot preserves, *Knott's®*

     Vanilla ice cream (optional)

1. Preheat oven to 400°F. Remove crusts from bread slices. Cut each slice in half diagonally; set aside. Drain pears, reserving ½ cup syrup.

2. In a pie plate, stir together 6 tablespoons of the melted butter and the reserved pear syrup. Dip bread triangles into butter mixture; use about two-thirds of the pieces to line the bottom and side of a 1½-quart casserole. Cut slices into smaller triangles to fill in.

3. In a medium skillet, combine pears, the remaining 2 tablespoons melted butter, the brown sugar, lemon juice, and pumpkin pie spice. Cook mixture over medium-high heat about 10 minutes or until pears break down, occasionally mashing with a fork. Remove from heat; stir in pecans and apricot preserves.

4. Spoon cooked fruit mixture over bread in casserole. Top with the remaining butter-dipped bread slices, filling in spaces with torn bread pieces.

5. Bake for 30 to 35 minutes or until top is toasted and browned. Serve warm with vanilla ice cream, if desired.

Apricot-Almond Caramel Tart

Prep 25 minutes   **Bake** 20 minutes + 25 minutes   **Oven** 350°F   **Makes** 8 servings

½   cup (1 stick) butter, softened

¼   cup sugar, *Domino®/C&H®*

½   cup finely crushed shortbread cookies, *Lorna Doone®*

½   cup all-purpose flour

⅔   cup chopped almonds, *Planters®*

⅓   cup chopped dried apricots, *Sunsweet®*

⅓   cup chopped dried figs, *Sun-Maid®*

⅓   cup cherry-flavor dried cranberries, *Craisins®*

⅓   cup golden raisins, *Sun-Maid®*

½   cup butterscotch caramel topping, *Mrs. Richardson's®*

1   can (15 ounces) apricot halves, drained, *Del Monte®*

½   cup frozen whipped dessert topping, thawed, *Cool Whip®*

½   teaspoon ground nutmeg, *McCormick®*

1. Preheat oven to 350°F. In a large mixing bowl, beat butter and sugar with an electric mixer on high until fluffy. Add shortbread crumbs and flour; beat on low about 5 seconds or until mixture comes together. Spread into the bottom and up sides of a 9-inch tart pan.

2. Bake for 20 to 25 minutes or until golden. Cool on a wire rack.

3. In a medium bowl, stir together almonds, dried apricots, figs, cranberries, and raisins.

4. In a small microwave-safe bowl, microwave caramel topping on high for 30 seconds. Pour over fruit mixture, stirring until combined. Spoon into shortbread crust. Top with apricot halves. Bake for 25 to 30 minutes or until filling is bubbly and pastry is golden. Cool completely on a wire rack.

5. For spiced cream, in a small bowl, gently combine whipped topping and nutmeg. Serve tart with spiced cream.

Toffee Coffee Tartlets

Prep 40 minutes   **Chill** 45 minutes   **Bake** according to package directions   **Makes** 6 servings

FILLING

- 1½ cups heavy cream
- ¼ cup brewed coffee, *Folgers® Classic Roast®*
- ¾ cup caramel topping, *Mrs. Richardson's®*
- 2 tablespoons butter

PASTRY CUPS

- 1 package (10 ounces) frozen puff pastry shells, *Pepperidge Farm®*
- ½ cup semisweet chocolate chips, *Nestlé®*
- ⅓ cup toffee bits, *Heath®*
- ½ cup powdered sugar, sifted, *Domino®/C&H®*

  Caramel topping, *Mrs. Richardson's®*

1. For filling, in a medium saucepan, stir together heavy cream and coffee. Bring to nearly boiling over medium heat; reduce heat to low. Heat coffee mixture for 5 minutes. Remove from heat. Using a fine-mesh wire strainer, strain coffee mixture into a small bowl; set aside.

2. Rinse out saucepan; heat the ¾ cup caramel topping over medium-high heat until boiling. Reduce heat to medium; cook for 2 minutes more. Remove from heat; stir in butter. Slowly stir in coffee-cream mixture until combined. Pour into a large mixing bowl; cool to room temperature. Chill in refrigerator about 45 minutes or until completely chilled.

3. For pastry cups, place puff pastry shells on an ungreased baking sheet; bake according to package instructions. Transfer to a wire rack; cool completely.

4. In a small microwave-safe bowl, microwave chocolate chips on medium about 1½ minutes or until melted, stirring every 30 seconds. Pour toffee bits into a pie plate. Dip top rim of pastry shells in melted chocolate, then in toffee bits; set aside.

5. Beat chilled coffee-cream mixture with an electric mixer on medium until it thickens. Slowly add powdered sugar, beating on high until stiff peaks form.

6. To serve, spoon coffee-cream mixture into a large zip-top plastic bag. Press out air; seal. Snip a small end off a corner of the bag; pipe coffee-cream mixture into shells.

7. Drizzle shells with additional caramel topping; serve immediately.

Orange-Pecan Balls

Prep 20 minutes   **Stand** 4 hours   **Makes** 14 balls

1   cup orange-flavor thin cookies, *Anna's®*

⅓   cup pecans, *Planters®*

¼   cup powdered sugar, sifted, *Domino®/C&H®*

2   tablespoons unsweetened cocoa powder, *Hershey's®*

2   tablespoons orange juice

1   tablespoon light-color corn syrup, *Karo®*

1. Place cookies in a food processor; cover and process to crumbs. Add pecans; pulse until mixture resembles fine crumbs. Pour into a medium bowl. Add powdered sugar and 1 tablespoon of the cocoa powder. Stir until combined. Add orange juice and corn syrup; stir until mixture comes together.

2. Pour the remaining 1 tablespoon cocoa powder into a pie plate. Scoop 1 tablespoon of the orange-syrup mixture; use your hands to form a smooth ball. Roll in cocoa powder, turning to coat entire ball; place on baking sheet. Repeat to make 14 balls. Cover loosely with plastic wrap; let stand for 4 hours before serving. Store balls in an airtight container at room temperature up to 3 days.

Hot Chocolate Floats

Start to Finish 15 minutes   **Makes** 2 servings

1½   cups milk

½   cup semisweet chocolate chips, *Nestle®*

2   tablespoons sugar

1   tablespoon plus 1 teaspoon unsweetened cocoa powder, *Hershey's®*

½   teaspoon ground cinnamon, *McCormick®*

4   scoops chocolate chip ice cream

2   scoops coconut sorbet

1   aerosol can refrigerated whipped dessert topping, *Cool Whip®*

4   chocolate wafer cookies, crushed, *Nabisco® Famous*

Dark chocolate, coarsely chopped

Tip: To save time when preparing this recipe for guests, scoop ice cream ahead of time and store the scoops on a parchment paper-lined baking sheet in your freezer until ready to serve.

1. In a small saucepan, combine milk, chocolate chips, sugar, cocoa powder, and cinnamon; cook and stir over medium-high heat until chocolate chips are melted and smooth. Remove from heat.

2. For each serving, fill a tall heatproof glass or mug with two scoops chocolate chip ice cream and one scoop coconut sorbet. Pour hot chocolate mixture over all. Top with whipped topping. Garnish with crushed cookies and chocolate. Serve immediately.

Pots de Crème

Prep 15 minutes   **Chill** 4 hours   **Makes** 4 servings

⅓   cup chocolate milk, *Nesquik®*

3   tablespoons butter, softened

3   tablespoons refrigerated liquid egg whites, *All Whites®*

2   tablespoons sugar, *Domino®/C&H®*

2   tablespoons chocolate syrup, *Hershey's®*

1   tablespoon unsweetened cocoa powder, *Hershey's®*

¼   cup heavy cream

1   cup semisweet chocolate chips, *Nestlé®*

1. In a blender, combine chocolate milk, butter, egg whites, sugar, chocolate syrup, and cocoa powder. Cover; blend until smooth.

2. In a small saucepan, heat cream over medium heat until almost boiling. Pour hot cream into blender. Scrape down side of blender. Add chocolate chips. Cover; blend until smooth.

3. Pour mixture into four 4-ounce ramekins. Cover each ramekin with plastic wrap. Chill in refrigerator about 4 hours or until set.

Crunchy Lemon Head Bark

Prep 20 minutes   **Chill** 1 hour + 2 hours   **Makes** 14 ounces

Nonstick cooking spray

1   package (12 ounces) semisweet chocolate chips, *Nestle®*

¼   cup lemon drops candy

1   bar (8 ounces) white baking chocolate, chopped, *Ghirardelli®*

2   teaspoons pure lemon oil, *Boyajian®*

5   to 6 drops yellow food coloring, *McCormick®*

1. Line a 13×9-inch baking pan with foil; spray with cooking spray; set aside.

2. In a medium microwave-safe dish, microwave chocolate chips on medium about 3 minutes or until melted, stirring every 1½ minutes.

3. Evenly spread a thin layer of the melted chocolate in the bottom of the prepared baking pan. Chill in the refrigerator about 1 hour or until firm.

4. Place lemon drops in a large zip-top plastic bag. Press out air; seal. With the back of a skillet, pound candy until crushed; set aside.

5. In a small microwave-safe dish, microwave chopped white chocolate on medium about 2 minutes or until melted, stirring every 30 seconds. Stir in lemon oil and yellow food coloring until combined.

6. Evenly spread white chocolate mixture in a thin layer over dark chocolate in baking pan. Sprinkle crushed lemon drops on top. Chill in the refrigerator about 2 hours or until set.

7. Break into pieces; store in an airtight container at room temperature up to 2 days or in the refrigerator for up to 1 week.

Sentimental Sweets

Sometimes the taste of a familar spice cake, jam-filled cookie, or brownie really hits the spot. These are the flavors food memories are built on, and they never grow old.

Orange-Raspberry Celebration Cake

Prep 25 minutes   **Bake** 35 minutes   **Oven** 350°F   **Makes** 10 servings

Nonstick cooking spray

1¼ cups water

7 tablespoons orange juice concentrate, thawed, *Minute Maid*®

1 package (18.25 ounces) butter-recipe yellow cake mix, *Betty Crocker*®

½ cup (1 stick) butter, softened

3 eggs

Orange icing coloring, *Wilton*® (or 2 drops red food coloring plus 5 drops yellow food coloring, *McCormick*®)

1 tablespoon light-color corn syrup, *Karo*®

½ cup hot water

1 package (3 ounces) raspberry gelatin, *Jell-O*®

12 ounces fresh raspberries

1 cup chopped glazed pecans, *Diamond of California*®

1 container (8 ounces) frozen whipped dessert topping, thawed, *Cool Whip*®

1. Preheat oven to 350°F. Spray two 8-inch round cake pans with cooking spray; set aside.

2. In a large mixing bowl, combine the 1¼ cups water and 5 tablespoons of the orange juice concentrate, stirring until concentrate is dissolved. Add cake mix, butter, eggs, and orange food coloring to bowl. Beat with an electric mixer on low for 30 seconds. Scrape down side of bowl; beat on medium for 2 minutes more. Pour batter into prepared pans.

3. Bake for 35 to 40 minutes or until a toothpick inserted near centers comes out clean. Cool in pans on a wire rack 10 minutes; remove from pans.

4. In a small bowl, stir together the remaining 2 tablespoons orange juice concentrate and the corn syrup; set aside.

5. In a small glass measuring cup, combine the ½ cup hot water and the gelatin, stirring until gelatin is dissolved.

6. To serve, place one cake layer on serving plate. Using a wooden skewer, poke holes into the top of the cake. Pour half the raspberry gelatin over cake layer. Arrange half the raspberries and half the pecans on top. Pour half the corn syrup mixture over fruit and nuts; top with half the whipped topping. Place the second cake layer on top; repeat layers.

Lemon Spice Marble Cake

Prep 25 minutes   **Bake** 40 minutes   **Oven** 350°F   **Makes** 12 servings

Nonstick cooking spray

½   cup self-rising flour

½   cup sugar, *Domino®/C&H®*

¼   cup (½ stick) butter, softened

4   eggs

¼   cup + 2 tablespoons lemonade concentrate, *Minute Maid®*

2   teaspoons lemon extract, *McCormick®*

10   drops yellow food coloring, *McCormick®*

1   cup water

1   package (18.25 ounces) spice cake mix, *Duncan Hines®*

1   cup vegetable oil

1. Preheat oven to 350°F. Spray a 10-inch fluted tube pan with cooking spray; set aside.

2. For lemon batter, in a medium mixing bowl, combine flour, sugar, butter, 1 egg, ¼ cup of the lemonade concentrate, the lemon extract, and yellow food coloring; beat with an electric mixer on low about 2 minutes or until batter thickens.

3. For spice batter, in a small bowl, stir the remaining 2 tablespoons lemonade concentrate into the water. In a large mixing bowl, combine the water mixture, the remaining 3 eggs, the spice cake mix, and oil; beat with electric mixer on low for 30 seconds. Scrape down the side of bowl; beat on medium for 2 minutes more.

4. Using half the lemon batter, drop spoonfuls into prepared tube pan. Pour spice batter over lemon batter in pan. Using a wooden skewer, swirl batters. Drop the remaining lemon batter by spoonfuls into the pan; swirl again with skewer.

5. Bake for 40 to 45 minutes or until a toothpick inserted near center of cake comes out clean. Cool cake in pan on a wire rack for 10 minutes. Remove cake from pan. Cool completely on wire rack.

Lemon Spice
Marble Cake
50¢/slice

Lemon-Filled Coconut Cupcakes

Prep 40 minutes **Bake** 15 minutes **Oven** 350°F **Makes** 24 cupcakes

1½ cups sweetened shredded coconut, *Baker's*®

1 package (18.25 ounces) yellow cake mix, *Duncan Hines*®

1½ cups coconut milk, *A Taste of Thai*®

3 eggs

1 package (4-serving-size) instant lemon pudding and pie filling mix, *Jell-O*®

⅓ cup vegetable oil

¼ teaspoon yellow food coloring, *McCormick*®

2 containers (12 ounces each) whipped whipped cream frosting, *Betty Crocker*®

¾ cup lemon curd, *Dickinson's*®

1 teaspoon imitation coconut extract, *McCormick*®

1. Preheat oven to 350°F. Line twenty-four 2½-inch muffin cups with paper baking cups; set aside.

2. Spread 1 cup of the coconut on a baking sheet. Toast for 6 to 8 minutes or until golden brown. Cool completely on wire rack.

3. In a large mixing bowl, combine cake mix, coconut milk, eggs, pudding mix, oil, and yellow food coloring; beat with an electric mixer on low for 30 seconds. Scrape down the side of bowl; beat on medium for 2 minutes more. Spoon batter into prepared muffin cups, filling each about three-fourths full.

4. Bake for 15 to 20 minutes or until a toothpick inserted near centers comes out clean. Cool cupcakes in muffin cups on a wire rack for 5 minutes. Remove cupcakes from muffin cups; cool completely on wire rack.

5. For lemon filling, in a medium bowl, stir together ½ cup of the whipped cream frosting and the lemon curd until combined.

6. With a sharp knife, make a ½-inch slit in the top center of each cooled cupcake. Place lemon filling in a disposable piping bag; snip a small end off one corner of the bag. Pipe filling into cupcakes.

7. In a medium bowl, stir coconut extract into the remaining whipped cream frosting; frost cupcakes.

8. Toss together toasted coconut and the remaining ½ cup untoasted coconut. Sprinkle coconut mixture over frosted cupcakes.

Coconut Macaroon Brownies

Prep 25 minutes   **Bake** 30 minutes + 15 minutes   **Oven** 350°F/375°F   **Makes** 12 brownies

Nonstick cooking spray

1   package (19.9 ounces) dark chocolate brownie mix, *Duncan Hines®*

½   cup vegetable oil

2   eggs

¼   cup chocolate milk, *Nesquik®*

⅓   cup miniature chocolate chips, *Nestlé®*

3   cups sweetened shredded coconut, *Baker's®*

¾   cup cream of coconut, *Coco Casa®*

4   egg whites

3   tablespoons cake flour, *Swans Down®*

Pinch salt

1. Preheat oven to 350°F. Spray a 9-inch square baking pan with cooking spray; set aside.

2. In a large bowl, stir together brownie mix, oil, eggs, and chocolate milk until combined. Stir in chocolate chips; pour mixture into the prepared baking pan.

3. Bake for 30 minutes. Remove from oven; increase oven temperature to 375°F.

4. In a medium saucepan, combine coconut, cream of coconut, egg whites, cake flour, and salt; cook and stir over medium heat about 5 minutes or until an instant-read thermometer inserted in mixture registers 120°F. Spoon hot coconut mixture over warm brownies.

5. Bake for 15 to 20 minutes more or until done in center and coconut edges are lightly toasted. Cool in pan on a wire rack.

Orange Almond Shortbread Cookies

Prep 25 minutes   **Chill** I hour   **Bake** 9 minutes per batch   **Oven** 350°F   **Makes** 48 cookies

4	ounces cream cheese, softened, *Philadelphia®*
¼	cup orange cappuccino mix, *General Foods® International*
I	egg
½	teaspoon almond extract, *McCormick®*
½	teaspoon orange extract, *McCormick®*
I	pouch (17.5 ounces) sugar cookie mix, *Betty Crocker®*
¾	cup almonds, toasted and ground, *Planters®*
6	tablespoons all-purpose flour
2	teaspoons finely shredded orange zest

1. For dough, in a large mixing bowl, beat cream cheese and cappuccino mix with an electric mixer on medium until smooth. Add egg, almond extract, and orange extract; beat until creamy. Add sugar cookie mix, almonds, flour, and orange zest, stirring until dough comes together. Divide dough in half; roll into two 2-inch-diameter logs. Wrap in plastic wrap; chill in refrigerator for at least I hour.

2. Preheat oven to 350°F. Line cookie sheets with parchment paper; set aside.

3. Slice logs into ¼-inch slices. Space slices 2 inches apart on prepared cookie sheets.

4. Bake for 9 to II minutes or until edges start to turn brown. Cool on cookie sheets for 5 minutes. Transfer cookies to a wire rack; cool completely.

Sweet Potato Squares

Prep 20 minutes   **Bake** 40 minutes   **Cool** 2 hours   **Oven** 350°F   **Makes** 12 servings

	Nonstick cooking spray
I	package (18.25 ounces) spice cake mix, *Duncan Hines®*
¾	cup (I½ sticks) butter, melted
I	can (19 ounces) cut sweet potatoes, *Princella®*
I	cup packed brown sugar, *Domino®/C&H®*
½	cup evaporated milk, *Carnation®*
2	eggs
I	tablespoon pumpkin pie spice, *McCormick®*
¾	cup chopped pecans, *Planters®*

1. Preheat oven to 350°F. Spray a 13×9-inch baking pan with cooking spray.

2. In a large bowl, combine 2 cups of the dry cake mix and ½ cup of the melted butter, stirring with a fork until mixture comes together. Press into bottom of prepared baking pan.

3. In a food processor, combine sweet potatoes, brown sugar, evaporated milk, eggs, and pumpkin pie spice. Process until smooth. Spread in pan.

4. In a small bowl, toss together the remaining dry cake mix, the remaining ¼ cup melted butter, and the pecans. Sprinkle on the sweet potato layer.

5. Bake for 40 to 45 minutes or until a toothpick inserted near center comes out clean. Cool in pan on a wire rack 2 hours before cutting into squares.

50¢

Orange Snaps with Cream Filling

Prep 30 minutes   **Chill** 1 hour   **Bake** 6 minutes per batch   **Oven** 350°F   **Makes** 18 sandwich cookies

COOKIES

6	tablespoons orange juice
1	package (14.5 ounces) gingerbread cake and cookie mix, *Krusteaz®*
2	tablespoons all-purpose flour
2	tablespoons butter, melted

FILLING

3	tablespoons meringue powder*
3	tablespoons light corn syrup, *Karo®*
1½	tablespoons orange juice
1½	cups powdered sugar, sifted, *Domino®/C&H®*
6	tablespoons vegetable shortening, *Crisco®*

1. Preheat oven to 350°F. Line cookie sheets with parchment paper; set aside.

2. In a large microwave-safe bowl, microwave the 6 tablespoons orange juice on high for 30 seconds. Stir in gingerbread mix, flour, and butter until dough comes together. (Add water, 1 teaspoon at a time, if necessary.) Roll dough into a 9-inch log; wrap in plastic wrap. Chill in refrigerator for at least 1 hour.

3. Slice log into ¼-inch slices. Shape slices into perfect circles; place 2 inches apart on prepared cookie sheets. Bake for 6 to 8 minutes or until edges are firm. Cool on cookie sheets on a wire rack for 5 minutes. Transfer cookies to wire rack; cool completely.

4. For filling, in a medium mixing bowl, beat meringue powder, corn syrup, and the 1½ tablespoons orange juice with an electric mixer on medium for 1 minute. Add powdered sugar and shortening, beating until combined. Spread 1 tablespoon of the filling on each of 18 of the orange snaps. Top with the remaining orange snaps to make 18 sandwich cookies.

*Note: Meringue powder is available at cake decorating stores, crafts stores, or online at wilton.com.

Chocolate Strawberry Hearts

Prep 35 minutes   **Chill** 30 minutes   **Bake** 7 minutes per batch   **Oven** 375°F   **Makes** 18 to 26 sandwich cookies

1   pouch (17.5 ounces) sugar cookie mix, *Betty Crocker*®

½   cup plus 1 tablespoon unsweetened cocoa powder, *Ghirardelli's*®

⅓   cup butter, softened

1   egg
     White, red, and pink sparkling sugar

½   cup strawberry jam, *Knott's*®

1. Preheat oven to 375°F. Line cookie sheets with parchment paper; set aside.

2. In a large bowl, stir together cookie mix, cocoa powder, butter, and egg until dough comes together. Shape mixture into a ball and wrap in plastic wrap. Chill in refrigerator for at least 30 minutes.

3. On a lightly floured surface, roll out dough to ¼-inch thickness. Using a 2½-inch heart-shape cookie cuter, cut out shapes. Reroll dough scraps and cut out more cookies until all the dough is used. Space half the cookies 2 inches apart on prepared cookie sheets. Bake for 7 to 9 minutes or until edges are firm and bottoms are light brown. Cool on cookie sheets on a wire rack for 5 minutes. Transfer cookies to wire rack; cool completely.

4. Using a 1¼-inch heart-shape cookie cutter, cut out the centers of the remaining cookies. Space cut-out hearts 2 inches apart on prepared cookie sheets. Arrange the heart centers on another prepared cookie sheet. Sprinkle with sparkling sugar. Bake for 6 to 8 minutes or until edges are firm and bottoms are light brown. Cool on cookie sheets on a wire rack for 5 minutes. Transfer cookies to a wire rack; cool completely.

5. Spoon about 1 teaspoon of the strawberry jam on each of the whole cookies. Top with cut-out cookies. Spread half the cut-out heart centers with some of the remaining jam; top with remaining cut-out heart centers to make tiny heart cookie sandwiches.

Fruit Fête

Enhancing fresh fruit with sugar, butter, or chocolate brings out its beauty and taste! Serve these fruity desserts warm, cold—or, sometimes, with ice cream.

Pear Crepes
in Boysenberry-Pear Sauce

Start to Finish 30 minutes   **Makes** 8 servings

2⅔   cups canned sliced pears in juice, *S&W*®

1   can (15 ounces) boysenberries in syrup, *Oregon*®

1   cup pear nectar

½   cup boysenberry jam, *Smucker's*®

2   teaspoons frozen lemon juice, thawed, *Minute Maid*®

2   containers (8 ounces each) mascarpone cheese, softened

2   teaspoons vanilla extract, *McCormick*®

¼   teaspoon ground allspice, *McCormick*®

8   (9 inches each) purchased crepes

1. Drain pears, reserving ¼ cup juice; set pears and reserved juice aside.

2. For sauce, in a small saucepan, combine undrained boysenberries, pear nectar, jam, and lemon juice; cook over medium-high heat until boiling. Reduce heat. Simmer until liquid is reduced to ½ cup. Using a fine-mesh strainer, strain mixture into a small bowl. Stir in reserved pear juice. Cool to room temperature.

3. In another small bowl, stir together mascarpone, vanilla, and allspice.

4. For each serving, place a crepe on a dessert plate; fold crepe in half. Spread about 2 tablespoons of the mascarpone mixture on one side of the crepe half; top with ⅓ cup of the pears. Fold a corner of the crepe over pears to make a triangle. Spoon 1 tablespoon of the boysenberry-pear sauce over crepe.

Mango-Blackberry Cassata

Prep 30 minutes   **Freeze** 1 hour + 4 hours   **Makes** 8 servings

1   cup vanilla meringue cookies, *Miss Meringue®*

2   cups vanilla bean ice cream, softened*

¾   cup blackberry jam, *Knott's®*

2   ounces cream cheese, softened and at room temperature, *Philadelphia®*

1   pint mango sorbet, softened*

1. Line the bottom and sides of a 8×4-inch loaf pan with plastic wrap, extending plastic wrap over the edges of the pan; set aside.

2. Place meringue cookies in a large zip-top plastic bag. Press out air; seal bag. Using a rolling pin, crush cookies into pieces; set aside.

3. Spread vanilla ice cream into bottom of prepared loaf pan. Freeze for 30 minutes.

4. In a small bowl, stir together blackberry jam and cream cheese until smooth. Spread mixture on top of ice cream. Freeze for 30 minutes more.

5. Spread sorbet on top of blackberry mixture. Top with meringue cookie pieces. Pull edges of plastic wrap over to cover; freeze for at least 4 hours.

6. To serve, uncover dessert. Lift dessert from pan by pulling up on edges of the plastic wrap. Slice and serve immediately.

*Note: Let the ice cream and sorbet stand at room temperature until it's soft but not melted.

Broiled Berries with Mascarpone

Start to Finish 30 minutes   **Makes** 6 servings

2   cups frozen mixed berries, thawed, *Dole*®

I   can (15 ounces) boysenberries, drained, *Oregon*®

I   can (15 ounces) red raspberries, drained, *Oregon*®

¼   cup blueberry syrup, *Smucker's*®

8   ounces mascarpone, softened

¼   cup powdered sugar, sifted, *Domino*®/*C&H*®

I   egg yolk

½   teaspoon almond extract, *McCormick*®

1. Preheat broiler. In a broilerproof 2-quart baking dish, gently stir together mixed berries, boysenberries, raspberries, and blueberry syrup.

2. In a medium bowl, stir together mascarpone, powdered sugar, egg yolk, and almond extract. Spoon mixture over berries in baking dish.

3. Broil 6 inches from the heat for 4 to 8 minutes or until cheese mixture starts to brown.

Plum Apricot Clafouti

Prep 30 minutes   **Bake** 40 minutes   **Oven** 325°F   **Makes** 8 servings

  Nonstick cooking spray

I   can (15 ounces) whole plums in heavy syrup, drained, *Oregon*®

I   cup pancake and waffle mix, *Aunt Jemima*®

½   cup sugar, *Domino*®/*C&H*®

½   teaspoon ground cinnamon, *McCormick*®

½   teaspoon ground nutmeg, *McCormick*®

½   cup milk

½   cup apricot nectar, *Kern's*®

4   eggs

I   teaspoon vanilla extract, *McCormick*®

I   can (15 ounces) apricot halves in syrup, drained, *Del Monte*®

  Frozen whipped dessert topping, thawed, *Cool Whip*®

1. Preheat oven to 325°F. Spray a 9½- to 10-inch glass pie plate with cooking spray; set aside. Cut plums in half and remove pits; set plums aside.

2. In a medium bowl, combine pancake mix, sugar, cinnamon, and nutmeg.

3. In a large bowl, whisk together milk, apricot nectar, eggs, and vanilla. Add pancake mixture, whisking until combined. Pour half the batter into prepared pie plate. Arrange plums and apricots on batter in pie plate, alternating fruits. Pour the remaining batter over fruit.

4. Bake for 40 to 45 minutes or until set in center. Cool in pan on a wire rack. Cut into wedges. Top each serving with whipped topping.

Blackberry Fool
with Chocolate Balsamic Drizzle

Start to finish 40 minutes   **Makes** 4 servings

2   cups frozen blackberries, *Dole®*

¼   cup sugar, *Domino®/C&H®*

3   cups frozen whipped dessert topping, thawed, *Cool Whip®*

6   tablespoons packed brown sugar, *Domino®/C&H®*

¼   cup balsamic vinegar

¼   teaspoon ground cinnamon, *McCormick®*

1   ounce bittersweet chocolate bar or dark chocolate bar, grated, *Ghirardelli®*

4   shortbread cookies, *Walkers®*

1. For blackberry fool, in a medium microwave-safe bowl, combine blackberries and sugar; microwave on defrost about 1 minute or until berries are defrosted. Transfer to a blender. Cover and blend about 10 seconds or until smooth. Pour into a large bowl; gently fold in whipped topping. Cover and refrigerate until ready to serve.

2. For chocolate balsamic sauce,* in a small saucepan, combine brown sugar, balsamic vinegar, and cinnamon; cook over medium-high heat until sugar is dissolved, whisking constantly. Reduce heat to medium; simmer for 5 minutes. Remove from heat; stir in grated chocolate.

3. To serve, dip one half of each shortbread in chocolate balsamic sauce; place on waxed paper to harden. Fill 4 dessert glasses with blackberry fool; drizzle each with chocolate balsamic sauce. Serve with chocolate-coated shortbread.

*Note: The chocolate balsamic sauce hardens at room temperature, so prepare the sauce just before serving the dessert.

Apricot and Boysenberry Summer Pudding

Prep 30 minutes   **Chill** 4 hours   **Makes** 6 servings

1   **can (15 ounces) apricot halves in extra-light syrup,** *Del Monte*®

¾   **cup boysenberry syrup,** *Smucker's*®

⅓   **cup dried apricots,** *Sun-Maid*®

¼   **cup sugar,** *Domino*®/*C&H*®

1   **tablespoon frozen lemon juice, thawed,** *Minute Maid*®

1   **package (12 ounces) butter loaf cake, sliced,** *Entenmann's*®

1   **can (15 ounces) boysenberries in light syrup, drained,** *Oregon*®

       Vanilla bean ice cream

1. In a medium saucepan, combine undrained apricot halves, ½ cup of the boysenberry syrup, the dried apricots, sugar, and lemon juice; cook over medium-high heat until boiling. Reduce heat. Simmer about 10 minutes or until half the liquid has evaporated.

2. Meanwhile, line bottom and sides of an 8×4-inch loaf pan with plastic wrap, extending plastic wrap over the edges of the pan. Line bottom and sides of the pan with cake slices, filling in any spaces with cake pieces.

3. Remove apricot mixture from heat; stir in boysenberries. Pour half the hot fruit mixture over cake in pan. Place 3 cake slices horizontally on top. Pour in the remaining fruit mixture; cover with 3 more cake slices. Pour the remaining ¼ cup boysenberry syrup over the entire dessert. Pull up plastic wrap and tightly cover the surface of the pudding. Place tightly sealed heavy jars on the plastic wrap to weigh down pudding. Chill in the refrigerator for at least 4 hours or overnight.

4. To serve, unwrap plastic wrap on top of the pan. Lift pudding from pan by pulling up on edges of the plastic wrap; invert pudding onto a serving platter. Slice and serve with vanilla bean ice cream.

Strawberry Island Upside-Down Cake

Prep 25 minutes   **Bake** 50 minutes   **Oven** 350°F   **Makes** 12 servings

Nonstick cooking spray

1   **can (20 ounces) crushed pineapple in juice, Dole®**

1   **can (21 ounces) strawberry pie filling, Comstock® or Wilderness®**

1   **package (18.25 ounces) lemon cake mix, Duncan Hines®**

1   **cup sweetened shredded coconut, Baker's®**

½   **cup chopped macadamia nuts, Diamond of California®**

½   **cup (1 stick) butter, cut into pieces**

Coconut sorbet (optional)

1. Preheat oven to 350°F. Spray a 13×9-inch baking pan with cooking spray. Drain pineapple, reserving juice; set aside.

2. In a medium bowl, combine strawberry pie filling and drained pineapple. Spread mixture into prepared pan. Sprinkle dry cake mix over top. Top with coconut and macadamia nuts. Pour the reserved pineapple juice on top; dot with butter pieces.

3. Bake for 50 to 55 minutes or until a toothpick inserted near center of cake layer comes out clean and fruit is bubbling. Cool in pan on a wire rack.

4. If desired, serve with coconut sorbet.

Chocolate Decadence

There are times—a romantic dinner, Valentine's Day bake sale, or girls' night in with your best friends—when only the rich, luxurious taste of chocolate will do.

Mocha Napoleons

Prep 50 minutes   **Bake** 18 minutes   **Cool** 1 hour   **Oven** 350°F   **Makes** 7 servings

Nonstick cooking spray

1   package (18.3 ounces) fudge brownie mix, *Duncan Hines*®

2   tablespoons instant espresso powder

½   cup (1 stick) butter, melted and cooled

3   eggs

¾   cup semisweet chocolate chips, *Nestlé*®

1   cup chocolate-flavor frozen whipped dessert topping, thawed, *Cool Whip*®

Unsweetened cocoa powder, *Hershey's*®

1. Preheat oven to 350°F. Spray a 15×10-inch baking pan with cooking spray; set aside.

2. In a large bowl, stir together brownie mix and espresso powder. Add butter and eggs; stir until well mixed. Pour batter into prepared baking pan.

3. Bake for 18 to 20 minutes or just until set in center. Cool in pan on a wire rack.

4. Using a 2-inch round cookie cutter as a guide, trace fourteen 2-inch circles on parchment paper. Turn over parchment paper and place on baking sheet; set aside.

5. In a medium microwave-safe bowl, microwave chocolate chips on medium about 2 minutes or until melted, stirring every 30 seconds.

6. Scoop melted chocolate into a small zip-top plastic bag. Press out air; seal bag. Cut a small hole in a corner of the bottom of the bag. Pipe overlapping zigzag patterns on each 2-inch circle until all chocolate is used. Place baking sheet in refrigerator to harden chocolate.

7. Using a 2½-inch round cookie cutter, cut 14 circles from the cooled brownie. Remove baking sheet with piped chocolate disks from refrigerator.

8. To serve, place a brownie circle on a serving plate. Top with about 1 tablespoon of the chocolate whipped topping and a piped chocolate disk. Repeat layers. Sprinkle with cocoa powder. Repeat with the remaining brownie circles, chocolate whipped topping, and chocolate disks to make 7 Napoleons.

Chocolate Mousse Meringue Tart

Prep 30 minutes   **Bake** I hour   **Cool** 2 hours   **Oven** 300°F   **Makes** I (9-inch) tart

2	egg whites
	Pinch cream of tartar, *McCormick®*
¼	cup superfine sugar, *Domino®/C&H®*
I	tablespoon unsweetened cocoa powder, *Hershey's®*
I	package (2.8 ounces) milk chocolate mousse mix, *Nestlé® European Style*
⅔	cup cold chocolate milk, *Nesquik®*
I	teaspoon vanilla extract, *McCormick®*
I½	cups chocolate frozen whipped dessert topping, *Cool Whip®*
	Shaved white chocolate

I. Preheat oven to 300°F.

2. For meringue, in a large mixing bowl, beat egg whites and cream of tartar with an electric mixer on medium until mixture has doubled in volume. Gradually add sugar and cocoa powder, beating on high until stiff, shiny peaks form. Spread meringue into bottom and up side of a 9-inch tart pan with a removable bottom.

3. Bake for I hour. Turn off oven; use a wooden spoon to prop open oven door. Leave meringue in oven for another hour. Cool in pan on a wire rack.

4. Meanwhile, in a medium mixing bowl, combine mousse mix, chocolate milk, and vanilla extract; beat with an electric mixer on medium for I minute. Beat on high about 2 minutes or until thickened and lighter in color. Cover with plastic wrap. Chill in refrigerator until serving time.

5. Just before serving, gently stir chocolate whipped topping into mousse mixture. Spoon into cooled meringue crust. Sprinkle with shaved white chocolate.

Brownie Thins

Prep I5 minutes   **Bake** 7 minutes per batch   **Cool** 5 minutes per batch   **Oven** 350°F   **Makes** 28 cookies

I	package (10.25 ounces) fudge brownie mix, *Duncan Hines®*
I	tablespoon instant espresso powder
I	egg
⅓	cup vegetable oil
	Powdered sugar, *Domino®/C&H®* (optional)

I. Preheat oven to 350°F. Line cookie sheet(s) with parchment paper; set aside.

2. In a large bowl, stir together brownie mix, espresso powder, egg, and oil until well mixed.

3. Drop a 2-teaspoon portion of the brownie batter onto prepared cookie sheet; using the back of a spoon, spread evenly into a 3-inch circle. Repeat with the remaining batter, spacing circles 2 inches apart on cookie sheet(s).

4. Bake for 7 to 9 minutes or just until set in center. Cool on cookie sheet(s) for 5 minutes. Transfer cookies to a wire rack; cool completely.

5. If desired, dust tops with powdered sugar.

Cocoa-Espresso Crumb Tart

Prep 30 minutes   **Bake** 8 minutes   **Chill** I hour   **Stand** 4 hours   **Oven** 450°F   **Makes** I (8-inch) tart

CRUST

I⅓ cups pie crust mix, *Betty Crocker*®

2   tablespoons unsweetened cocoa powder, *Hershey's*®

2   tablespoons packed brown sugar, *Domino*®/*C&H*®

I   tablespoon instant espresso powder

2   tablespoons plus 2 teaspoons chocolate milk, *Nesquik*®

FILLING

I   package (12 ounces) semisweet chocolate chips, *Nestle*®

I   cup heavy cream

2   tablespoons packed brown sugar, *Domino*®/*C&H*®

¼   teaspoon almond extract, *McCormick*®

TOPPING

6   milk chocolate chunk macadamia nut cookies,* *Pepperidge Farm*® *Sausalito*®

I   tablespoon packed brown sugar, *Domino*®/*C&H*®

I   teaspoon unsweetened cocoa powder, *Hershey's*®

½   teaspoon instant espresso powder

I. For crust, preheat oven to 450°F. In a medium bowl, combine pie crust mix, the 2 tablespoons cocoa powder, 2 tablespoons brown sugar, the I tablespoon espresso powder, and the chocolate milk, stirring until dough comes together. Shape dough into a ball. Turn out dough onto a lightly floured surface. Roll dough from center to edge into a 9-inch-diameter circle; fit dough circle into an 8-inch tart pan. Prick bottom of crust with a fork. Bake for 8 to 10 minutes or until lightly browned. Cool completely.

2. For filling, place chocolate chips in a medium bowl; set aside. In a small saucepan, combine cream, 2 tablespoons brown sugar, and the almond extract; cook and stir over medium heat until nearly boiling. Pour over the chocolate chips; stir until smooth. Chill in refrigerator for I hour. Spread chocolate filling into cooled crust.

3. For topping, in a large zip-top plastic bag, combine cookies, the I tablespoon brown sugar, the I teaspoon cocoa powder, and the ½ teaspoon espresso powder. Press out air; seal bag. Using a rolling pin, roll over cookies until crumbly with some large chunks. Shake bag until mixture is combined. Sprinkle mixture over chocolate filling. For a creamy filling, let stand at room temperature about 4 hours or until set. For a thicker filling, chill in refrigerator for at least 2 hours.

***Note:** You can substitute other large chocolate chunk cookies for the *Sausalito*® cookies.

Dark Chocolate-Raspberry Truffles

Prep 50 minutes   **Chill** 2 hours   **Freeze** 1 hour   **Makes** 12 truffles

1   package (12 ounces) semisweet chocolate chips, *Nestle*®
1   cup heavy cream
½   teaspoon imitation raspberry extract, *McCormick*®
1   bottle (7.25 ounces) *Magic Shell*®, *Smucker's*®

1. Line a baking sheet with parchment paper; set aside. Place a wire rack on a second baking sheet; set aside.

2. Place chocolate chips in a medium bowl; set aside. In a small saucepan, combine cream and raspberry extract; heat over medium heat until nearly boiling. Pour over chocolate chips; stir until smooth. Cover with plastic wrap and chill in refrigerator about 2 hours or until mixture hardens.

3. Using a 2-tablespoon scoop, scoop chocolate-raspberry portions; place on parchment-lined baking sheet. Freeze for 1 hour.

4. Transfer chocolate-raspberry scoops to the wire rack over baking sheet. Drizzle *Magic Shell*® over each until completely covered. Return to freezer until ready to serve.

S'mores Fudge

Prep 35 minutes   **Bake** 15 minutes   **Cool** 15 minutes + 1 hour   **Chill** 2 hours   **Oven** 350°F   **Makes** 24 pieces

12   tablespoons (1½ sticks) butter
1½   cups graham cracker crumbs, *Honey Maid*®
2   cups plus 3 tablespoons sugar, *Domino*®/*C&H*®
1   cup evaporated milk, *Carnation*®
4   cups tiny marshmallows, *Kraft*® *Jet-Puffed*®
3¼   cups miniature milk chocolate bars, unwrapped, *Hershey's*®

1. Preheat oven to 350°F. Spray a 9×13-inch baking pan with cooking spray; set aside.

2. For graham crust, in a large microwave-safe bowl, microwave 6 tablespoons of the butter on high about 1 minute or until melted. Add graham cracker crumbs and the 3 tablespoons sugar, stirring with a fork until mixture comes together. Press into the bottom of the prepared baking pan.

3. Bake graham crust for 15 minutes. Cool in pan on a wire rack.

4. Meanwhile, in a large saucepan, combine the remaining 6 tablespoons butter, the remaining 2 cups sugar, and the evaporated milk. Cook and stir over medium heat until boiling; boil for 10 minutes, stirring occasionally.

5. Remove from heat. Add 3 cups of the marshmallows and 3 cups of the miniature chocolate bars, stirring until smooth. Cool at room temperature for 15 minutes.

6. Sprinkle the remaining 1 cup marshmallows over the cooled graham crust. Pour the cooked mixture over the marshmallows in baking pan. Press the remaining ¼ cup miniature chocolate bars into the top of the fudge, spacing bars evenly. Cool at room temperature for 1 hour. Chill in refrigerator about 2 hours or until set.

Chocolate Pistachio Biscotti

Prep 30 minutes   **Bake** 25 minutes per batch + 15 minutes per batch   **Oven** 350°F   **Makes** 18 biscotti

1   package (19.5 ounces) dark chocolate cake mix, *Duncan Hines*®

½   cup plus ⅓ cup finely chopped pistachio nuts, *Planters*®

1   package (7 ounces) almond paste, *Odense*®

½   cup (1 stick) cold butter

1   egg

2   egg whites

12   ounces semisweet chocolate bar or white chocolate bar, broken into pieces, *Ghirardelli*®

1. Preheat oven to 350°F. Line two baking sheets with parchment paper; set aside.

2. In a large bowl, stir together cake mix and the ½ cup pistachio nuts. Using a grater, grate almond paste and cold butter into cake mix mixture; gently toss to distribute evenly. In a medium mixing bowl, beat egg and egg whites with an electric mixer on medium until foamy. Pour eggs into cake mix mixture; stir until a sticky dough forms.

3. Turn out dough onto a lightly floured working surface. Shape into two rectangular loaves. Place each loaf in the center of a prepared baking sheet. Bake for 25 to 30 minutes or until a toothpick inserted into centers comes out clean.

4. Using a serrated knife, cut each loaf in ¾-inch slices. Arrange slices on same baking sheets, evenly spacing slices. Bake for 15 minutes more. Transfer to a wire rack; cool completely.

5. In a medium microwave-safe bowl, microwave chocolate chips on medium about 2½ minutes or until melted, stirring every 30 seconds. Spread tops of biscotti with a thin layer of melted chocolate; sprinkle with the remaining ⅓ cup pistachio nuts. Lay biscotti flat; let stand until chocolate hardens.

Chocolate-Banana Mini Loaves

Prep 20 minutes   **Bake** 35 minutes   **Cool** 20 minutes   **Oven** 400°F   **Makes** 2 mini loaves

Nonstick coking spray

¾   cup banana chips

1   package (17.1 ounces) banana nut muffin mix, *Krusteaz®*

¼   cup unsweetened cocoa powder, *Hershey's®*

¾   cup chocolate milk, *Nesquik®*

¼   cup vegetable oil

2   eggs

¾   cup semisweet chocolate chips, *Nestle®*

¾   cup powdered sugar, sifted, *Domino®/C&H®*

1½   tablespoons heavy cream

1   teaspoon imitation banana extract, *McCormick®*

1. Preheat oven to 400°F. Spray two 6×3-inch miniature loaf pans with cooking spray; set aside.

2. Place banana chips in a large zip-top plastic bag. Press out air; seal bag. Using a rolling pin, roll over chips until crushed; set aside.

3. In a large bowl, whisk together banana muffin mix and cocoa powder. Add chocolate milk, oil, and eggs, stirring until smooth (mixture will be thick). Stir in chocolate chips and banana chips. Divide batter evenly among miniature loaf pans.

4. Bake for 35 to 40 minutes or until a toothpick inserted in centers comes out clean. Cool in pans on wire rack for 20 minutes.

5. For glaze, in a small bowl, stir together powdered sugar, heavy cream, and banana extract until a glaze consistency. Drizzle glaze over loaves. Cool completely.

White Chocolate
Brownie-Bottom Cheesecake

Prep 30 minutes   **Bake** 30 minutes + 15 minutes   **Cool** 2 hours   **Chill** 4 hours   **Oven** 350°F   **Makes** 10 servings

Nonstick cooking spray

1   **package (19.9 ounces) dark chocolate brownie mix, *Duncan Hines*®**

½   **cup vegetable oil**

¼   **cup chocolate milk, *Nesquik*®**

3   **eggs**

½   **cup miniature chocolate chips, *Nestlé*®**

2½   **packages (8 ounces each) cream cheese, *Philadelphia*®**

1   **cup heavy cream**

¼   **cup sugar, *Domino*®/*C&H*®**

1   **package (4-serving-size) instant white chocolate pudding and pie filling mix, *Jell-O*®**

1   **bar (4 ounces) white chocolate baking bar, melted, *Ghirardelli*®**

½   **cup chocolate syrup, *Hershey's*®**

1. Fill a large roasting pan with boiling water; place pan on the bottom rack of the oven. Preheat oven to 350°F. Spray a 9-inch springform pan with cooking spray; set aside.

2. In a large bowl, combine brownie mix, oil, chocolate milk, and 2 of the eggs; stir until well mixed. Stir in miniature chocolate chips. Pour into prepared springform pan. Place on middle oven rack; bake for 30 minutes.

3. Meanwhile, in a large mixing bowl, beat cream cheese and cream with an electric mixer on low until smooth. Add sugar and pudding mix; beat until well mixed. Add the remaining egg; beat until combined, scraping down side of bowl.

4. Drop spoonfuls of the cheesecake mixture around the perimeter of the brownie mixture in pan. Spread the mixture toward the center of the pan until it forms an even layer. Bake for 15 to 20 minutes more or until cheesecake top is set but slightly jiggly in center.

5. Cool for 2 hours in pan on a wire rack. Chill in refrigerator for at least 4 hours. To serve, remove from pan. Drizzle each serving with melted white chocolate and chocolate syrup.

Candied Creations

Show your affection with a homemade confection! The bite-size goodies in this collection deliver big impact for taste and prettiness.

Truffle
Trio
$2.00

Florentine Minis

Prep 40 minutes   **Bake** 10 minutes   **Cool** 15 minutes   **Oven** 375°F   **Makes** 18 candies

6	tablespoons butter
6	tablespoons powdered sugar, *Domino®/C&H®*
1/4	cup sliced almonds, *Planters®*
1/4	cup pumpkin seeds
1/4	cup sweetened dried cranberries, finely chopped, *Craisins®*
1/4	cup dried apricots, finely chopped, *Sun-Maid®*
2	tablespoons heavy cream
3/4	cup semisweet chocolate chips, *Nestlé®*
18	chocolate wafer cookies, *Nabisco® Famous*

1. Preheat oven to 375°F. Line two baking sheets with parchment paper. Using a 2¼-inch round cookie cutter as a guide, trace 9 circles on each piece of parchment, evenly spacing circles.

2. In a medium saucepan, combine butter and powdered sugar; cook over medium-high heat until boiling. Add almonds, pumpkin seeds, cranberries, apricots, and cream; stir until well mixed. Remove from heat. Scoop 1 teaspoon of the mixture into center of a circle on baking sheet. Do not fill entire circle because mixture will spread during baking.*

3. Bake for 10 to 12 minutes or just until edges start to brown. Transfer to a wire rack; let stand for 15 minutes.

4. Meanwhile, in a small microwave-safe bowl, microwave chocolate chips on medium about 1½ minutes or until melted and smooth, stirring every 30 seconds.

5. To assemble, spread 1 teaspoon of the melted chocolate on a wafer cookie. Peel a cooled nut and fruit round from the parchment paper; place on the melted chocolate on the wafer cookie. Repeat to make 18 stacks.

*Note: If the nut and fruit mixture spreads too much during baking time, use the 2¼-inch round cookie cutter to cut a circle of the cooled nut and fruit mixture; peel from parchment paper and fit on the wafer cookie.

Pecan-Coconut Cookie Cups

Prep 30 minutes   **Bake** 10 minutes   **Oven** 350°F   **Makes** 34 cookie cups

FILLING

Nonstick cooking spray

¼ cup (½ stick) butter

½ cup plus 2 tablespoons sweetened condensed milk, *Eagle Brand*®

2 tablespoons brown sugar corn syrup, *Karo*®

Pinch salt

½ cup chopped pecans, *Planters*®

¼ cup sweetened shredded coconut, *Baker's*®

½ teaspoon imitation coconut extract, *McCormick*®

COOKIE CUPS

1 egg

1 pouch (17.5 ounces) rainbow chocolate candy cookie mix, *Betty Crocker*®

⅓ cup butter, softened

1. Preheat oven to 350°F. Spray thirty-four 1¾-inch muffin cups and the back of a tablespoon measuring spoon with cooking spray; set aside.

2. For filling, in a medium saucepan, melt butter over medium-high heat. Add sweetened condensed milk, corn syrup, and salt; bring to a boil. Boil for 2 minutes, stirring occasionally. Remove from heat. Stir in pecans, coconut, and coconut extract. Let stand at room temperature until ready to fill cups.

3. For cookie cups, spoon cookie mix into a wire-mesh strainer set over a large bowl. Sift cookie mix through strainer, leaving candy in strainer (reserve candy for another use). Add butter and egg to cookie mix in bowl; stir until combined. Spoon 2 teaspoons of the cookie dough into each prepared muffin cup. Using the back of the sprayed measuring spoon, press dough into bottoms and up sides of the cups.

4. Bake for 6 to 8 minutes or until set. Remove from oven. Immediately press each cup again with the back of the measuring spoon. Fill each cup with a heaping teaspoon of the filling. Bake for 4 to 6 minutes more or until filling is set. Cool in muffin cups on a wire rack. Carefully remove cookie cups from muffin cups.

Ginger Sorbet Cups

Prep 30 minutes   **Bake** 10 minutes   **Oven** 350°F   **Makes** 20 cups

Nonstick cooking spray

28   gingersnap cookies, *Nabisco®*

½   cup packed brown sugar, *Domino®/C&H®*

¼   cup cake flour, *Swans Down®*

¼   cup (½ stick) butter, melted

1   egg white

Lemon sorbet and/or mango sorbet

1. Preheat oven to 350°F. Spray twenty 1¾-inch muffin cups with cooking spray; set aside.

2. In a food processor, combine gingersnap cookies, brown sugar, and cake flour; cover and process until mixture forms fine crumbs. Add melted butter and egg white; pulse until mixture is well mixed.

3. Spoon a heaping tablespoonful of the mixture into each prepared muffin cup. Using the back of a measuring tablespoon, firmly press into bottoms and up sides of cups to make 20 cups.

4. Bake for 8 minutes. Remove from oven. Immediately press each cup again with the back of the measuring spoon. Bake for 2 to 4 minutes more or until set. Cool in muffin cups on a wire rack.

5. Using a 2-tablespoon ice cream scoop, fill each cooled ginger cup with a small scoop of the sorbet.*

*Note: You can scoop the sorbet into 2-tablespoon balls ahead of time and store on parchment paper-lined baking sheets in the freezer until you're ready to serve the cups.

Black Forest Brownie Cups

Prep 30 minutes   **Bake** 20 minutes + 15 minutes   **Chill** 5 minutes   **Oven** 350°F   **Makes** 18 cups

Nonstick cooking spray

1   package (10.25 ounces) fudge brownie mix, *Duncan Hines*®

⅓   cup butter, cut into tiny pieces

1   egg

¾   cup cherry pie filling, *Comstock*® or *Wilderness*®

¾   cup frozen whipped dessert topping, thawed, *Cool Whip*®

Unsweetened cocoa powder, *Hershey's*®

1. Preheat oven to 350°F. Spray eighteen 1¾-inch muffin cups with cooking spray; set aside.

2. In a large bowl, stir together brownie mix, butter pieces, and egg until well mixed. (Mixture should be thick; chill in refrigerator if necessary.)

3. Scoop 1 tablespoon of the brownie mixture into a prepared muffin cup. Using the back of a measuring tablespoon, press mixture into bottom and up sides of the cups to make 18 cups.

4. Bake for 20 minutes. Remove from oven; chill in the refrigerator about 5 minutes or until centers of brownie cups sink. Fill each sunken center with 2 teaspoons of the cherry pie filling.

5. Bake for 15 to 17 minutes or until a toothpick inserted into the brownie cups comes out almost clean. Cool in muffin cups on a wire rack.

6. Carefully remove brownie cups from muffin cups. Top each brownie cup with 2 teaspoons of the whipped topping. Dust with cocoa powder.

Caramel-Apple Muffin Melts

Prep 20 minutes   **Bake** 18 minutes   **Cool** 10 minutes   **Oven** 400°F   **Makes** 12 muffins

1	package (19 ounces) apple cinnamon muffin mix (with apple packet), *Krusteaz®*
1¼	cups apple juice, *Tree Top®*
1	teaspoon ground cinnamon, *McCormick®*
12	individual caramels, unwrapped, *Brach's® Milk Maid®*

1. Preheat oven to 400°F. Line twelve 2½-inch muffin cups with paper baking cups; set aside.

2. In a large bowl, stir together muffin mix with apple packet, apple juice, and cinnamon until combined. Spoon batter into prepared muffin cups, filling each cup three-fourths full.

3. Press a caramel into center of the batter in each muffin cup.

4. Bake for 18 to 20 minutes or until a toothpick inserted off-center in each muffin comes out clean. (Insert toothpick off-center to avoid caramel.)

5. Cool in muffin cups on a wire rack for 10 minutes for an oozing caramel effect. (Or cool 10 minutes; remove from muffin cups and cool completely for a soft caramel center.)

Angel Cupcake Minis

Prep 30 minutes   **Bake** 13 minutes   **Cool** 10 minutes   **Oven** 350°F   **Makes** 72 mini cupcakes

1   **package (16 ounces) angel food cake mix,** *Duncan Hines*®

1¼   **cups chilled white grape juice,*** *Welch's*®

1½   **cups whipped fluffy white frosting,**** *Duncan Hines*®

1½   **teaspoons extract of your choice,**** *McCormick*®

     Food coloring,** *McCormick*®

     Assorted sprinkles, colored sparkling sugars, and chocolate-covered sunflower seeds

1. Preheat oven to 350°F. Line seventy-two 1¾-inch muffin cups with miniature paper baking cups; set aside.

2. In a large mixing bowl, beat cake mix and white grape juice with an electric mixer on low for 30 seconds. Scrape side of bowl. Beat for 1 minute on medium. Spoon 1 tablespoon of the batter into each prepared muffin cup.

3. Bake for 13 to 16 minutes or until a toothpick inserted in centers comes out clean. Cool in muffin cups on a wire rack for 10 minutes. Remove from muffin cups; cool completely on wire rack.

4. In a small microwave-safe bowl, microwave frosting on high for 30 seconds or until a pourable consistency. Stir in extract and food coloring until well mixed.

5. Dip top of each angel cupcake into frosting mixture; turn upright. Sprinkle with assorted sprinkles or sparkling sugar, or decorate with chocolate-covered sunflower seeds.

*Note: You can substitute any flavor fruit nectar, *Kern's*®, for the white grape juice. (Or for adults, use ¾ cup any flavor fruit nectar plus ½ cup champagne instead of the white grape juice.)

**Note: If you prefer, omit the frosting, extract, and food coloring; frost the cupcakes with a milk chocolate ganache. For the ganache, place 1 cup milk chocolate chips in a small bowl. In a 1-cup glass measuring cup, microwave ½ cup heavy cream on high for 45 seconds. Pour hot cream over chocolate chips in bowl; stir until smooth. Dip tops of cupcakes in ganache; turn upright.

Pecan Cookie Turtles®

Prep 40 minutes   **Bake** 10 minutes   **Oven** 375°F   **Makes** 33 pieces

1   pouch (17.5 ounces) double chocolate chunk cookie mix, *Betty Crocker®*

¼   cup vegetable oil

2   tablespoons chocolate milk, *Nesquik®*

1   egg

165   whole pecans, *Planters®*

33   individual caramel candies, unwrapped and each shaped into a flat round disk, *Kraft®*

1. Preheat oven to 375°F. Line baking sheet(s) with parchment paper.

2. Spoon cookie mix into a wire-mesh strainer set over a large bowl. Sift cookie mix through strainer, leaving chocolate chips in strainer. Transfer chocolate chips to a small microwave-safe bowl; set aside. Add oil, chocolate milk, and egg to cookie mix in bowl, stirring until well mixed.

3. Arrange pecans in groups of 5 on prepared baking sheet, spacing pecan groups 1 inch apart and arranging each group to resemble a head and 4 legs with a quarter-size opening in the center. Drop 2 teaspoons of the cookie dough in the middle of each group of pecans. Repeat to fit as many on a baking sheet as possible.

4. Bake for 5 minutes. Remove from oven. Place a caramel disk on top of each cookie. Bake for 5 to 7 minutes more or until starting to brown. Transfer cookies to a wire rack; cool completely.

5. Microwave reserved chocolate chips on medium about 1½ minutes or until melted and smooth, stirring halfway through heating time.

6. Pour melted chocolate into a disposable piping bag; snip a small end off the bag. Pipe a crisscross pattern on each caramel for the turtle's shell. Pipe 2 dots on each turtle's head for eyes.

Peanut Butter Toffee Truffles

Prep 50 minutes   **Cool** 1 hour + 1 hour   **Makes** 15 truffles

1½   cups peanut butter and milk chocolate chips, *Nestlé®*

½   cup sweetened condensed milk, *Eagle Brand®*

1   teaspoon vanilla extract, *McCormick®*

¾   cup toffee bits, *Heath®*

1. In a small saucepan, combine chips and sweetened condensed milk; heat over medium until melted and smooth, stirring constantly. Pour into a small bowl. Stir in vanilla extract. Cool to room temperature. Cover with plastic wrap. Chill in refrigerator for 1 hour.

2. Pour toffee bits into a pie plate. Scoop 1 tablespoon of the peanut butter mixture into your slightly wet hands; form into a smooth ball. Roll ball in toffee bits, turning to coat entire ball. Place on prepared baking sheet. Repeat to make 15 balls, rinsing hands when mixture becomes too sticky to roll. Chill in refrigerator for 1 hour. Serve chilled or at room temperature.

Note: To store truffles, layer between pieces of waxed paper in an airtight container. Cover; seal. Truffles will keep for 3 to 4 days at room temperature, 1 week in the refrigerator, or up to 3 months in the freezer.

White Chocolate Peppermint Truffles

Prep I hour   **Chill** I hour   **Freeze** I hour   **Makes** I4 truffles

Nonstick cooking spray

6   tablespoons butter, softened

2   cups powdered sugar, sifted, *Domino®/C&H®*

2   tablespoons water

¼   teaspoon peppermint extract, *McCormick®*

I½   bars (4 ounces each; 6 ounces total) white chocolate baking bar, *Ghirardelli®*

7   peppermint starlight mints, crushed, *Brach's® Star Brites®*

1. Spray a baking sheet with cooking spray; set aside.

2. In a large mixing bowl, beat butter with an electric mixer on medium about I minute or until fluffy. Add half the powdered sugar, the water, and peppermint extract. Beat on low for 30 seconds. Add the remaining powdered sugar; beat until smooth. Cover with plastic wrap; chill in refrigerator for I hour.

3. Scoop I tablespoon of the peppermint mixture into your slightly wet hands; form into a smooth ball. Place on prepared baking sheet. Repeat to make I4 balls, rinsing hands when mixture becomes too sticky to roll. Chill in freezer for I hour.

4. In a small microwave-safe bowl, microwave white chocolate bar on medium for I½ minutes or until melted and smooth, stirring every 30 seconds. Using a fork, spear a peppermint ball; hold over the bowl of melted white chocolate. Using a spoon, drizzle the melted white chocolate over ball until well coated. Carefully slide truffle back onto baking sheet. Sprinkle truffle with crushed starlight mints. Repeat with the remaining peppermint balls. Chill in refrigerator until ready to serve.

Note: To store truffles, layer between pieces of waxed paper in an airtight container. Cover; seal. Truffles will keep for I week in the refrigerator or up to 3 months in the freezer.

Coco-Cabana Truffles

Prep 50 minutes   **Chill** 2 hours   **Makes** 40 truffles

2½   cups semisweet chocolate chips, *Nestlé®*

½   cup coconut milk, *Chaokoh®*

¼   cup banana syrup, *Margie's®*

2   teaspoons rum extract, *McMormick®*

I½   teaspoons imitation banana extract, *McCormick®*

2½   cups sweetened shredded coconut, *Baker's®*

1. Place chocolate chips in a medium bowl; set aside. In a small saucepan, combine coconut milk and banana syrup; cook over medium heat until nearly boiling. Pour coconut milk mixture over chocolate chips; stir until smooth. Stir in rum extract and banana extract until well mixed. Cover with plastic wrap. Chill in refrigerator for 2 hours.

2. Scoop 2 teaspoons of the chocolate mixture into your slightly wet hands; form into a smooth ball. Roll ball in coconut, turning to coat entire ball. Place on a baking sheet. Repeat to make 40 balls, rinsing hands when mixture becomes too sticky to roll. Chill in freezer until ready to serve.

Note: To store truffles, layer between pieces of waxed paper in an airtight container. Cover; seal. Truffles will keep for I week in the refrigerator or up to 3 months in the freezer.

White Chocolate
Peppermint Truffles

Coco-Cabana Truffles

Peanut Butter Toffee Truffles,
recipe page 166

Pies & Pastries

Topped with fresh fruit, rich cheesecake, light-as-air mousse, or creamy custard, a flaky crust is irresistible. Fill a crust and you've made a sale.

Peach Crumble Pies

Prep 30 minutes   **Bake** 10 minutes + 50 minutes   **Cool** 1 hour   **Oven** 425°F/375°F   **Makes** 2 (9-inch) pies

1	package (20 ounces) pie crust mix, *Krusteaz®*
1/3	cup plus 6 tablespoons peach nectar, *Kern's®*
1/4	cup peach-flavor gelatin, *Jell-O®*
2	cans (21 ounces each) peach pie filling, *Comstock®* or *Wilderness®*
1	package (21 ounces) cinnamon crumb cake mix, *Krusteaz®*
1¼	cups chopped walnuts, *Planters®*
¾	cup (1½ sticks) cold butter, cut into pieces

1. Preheat oven to 425°F. Line a baking sheet with foil; set aside.

2. In a medium bowl, combine pie crust mix and the 1/3 cup peach nectar, stirring until dough comes together. (If needed, add more peach nectar, 1 teaspoon at a time.) Roll into a ball; turn out onto a lightly floured surface. Divide dough into two balls. Roll one dough ball into a 10-inch-diameter circle; fit circle into a 9-inch pie pan. Crimp edges of pie dough; prick bottom of the crust with a fork. Repeat with the remaining dough ball.

3. Bake both crusts for 10 to 15 minutes or until lightly browned. Cool in pans on wire racks. Reduce oven temperature to 375°F.

4. In a small microwave-safe bowl, microwave the remaining 6 tablespoons peach nectar on high for 1 minute. Add dry peach gelatin, stirring until dissolved. In a large bowl, stir together pie filling and gelatin mixture. Pour half of the mixture into each of the cooled pie crusts.

5. In a medium bowl, stir together crumb cake mix and walnuts. Using a pastry blender, cut in butter until mixture is crumbly with some large chunks. Sprinkle half the crumb mixture on each of the pies.*

6. Place pies on prepared baking sheet. Bake for 50 to 60 minutes or until crumble is golden brown, breaking up crumb mixture with a fork halfway through baking time. Cool in pans on wire racks.

***Note:** If desired, freeze one of the unbaked pies. To serve, thaw the pie overnight in refrigerator. Bake as directed in Step 6.

Peach Crumble
Pie $8.00

Triple Blueberry Pie

Prep 30 minutes   **Bake** 15 minutes + 20 minutes + 30 minutes   **Cool** 1 hour   **Oven** 425°F/325°F   **Makes** 1 (9-inch) pie

2   **(9 inches each) frozen unbaked deep-dish pastry shells, thawed,** *Marie Callender's*®

1   **can (21 ounces) blueberry pie filling,** *Comstock*® **or** *Wilderness*®

1   **cup frozen blueberries,** *Dole*®

½   **cup dried blueberries,** *Mariani*®

¼   **cup sugar,** *Domino*®/*C&H*®

3   **tablespoons cornstarch**

¾   **teaspoon almond extract,** *McCormick*®

1   **egg**

      Sugar, *Domino*®/*C&H*®

1. Preheat oven to 425°F. Line a baking sheet with foil; set aside.

2. Remove one of the pastry shells from pie pan and place on lightly floured surface; set aside. Prick the bottom of the other pastry shell with a fork; place on prepared baking sheet. Bake for 15 to 20 minutes or until golden brown. Cool in pan on a wire rack.

3. In a large bowl, stir together pie filling, frozen blueberries, dried blueberries, sugar, cornstarch, and ½ teaspoon of the almond extract. Pour into cooled crust.

4. In a small bowl, lightly beat together egg and the remaining ¼ teaspoon almond extract. Using a pastry brush, brush egg mixture on edge of baked crust.

5. Using a heart-shape cookie cutter, cut 3 heart shapes in the other pie shell. Place crust on top of the pie filling mixture; crimp edges of crusts together. Place heart cutouts on top of the crust in desired pattern. Brush egg mixture over the top of the pie crust. Sprinkle with sugar. Place pie on prepared baking sheet.

6. Bake for 20 minutes. Reduce oven temperature to 325°F; bake for 30 to 40 minutes more or until fruit is bubbling and crust is golden brown. (If edges brown too quickly, cover with foil.) Cool in pan on wire rack.

Coco Mocha Pie

Prep 30 minutes   **Cool** 1 hour   **Chill** 3 hours   **Makes** 1 (9-inch) pie

1   (9 inches) frozen unbaked deep-dish pastry shell, *Marie Callender's*®

1¼   cups light coconut milk, *Thai Kitchen*®

½   cup double-strength brewed coffee, cooled

2   tablespoons sugar, *Domino*®/*C&H*®

1   teaspoon imitation rum extract, *McCormick*®

1   cup instant vanilla pudding and pie filling mix,* *Jell-O*®

1   cup sweetened shredded coconut, *Baker's*®

1   container (8 ounces) frozen whipped dessert topping, thawed, *Cool Whip*®

¼   cup sweetened shredded coconut, toasted, *Baker's*®

1. Bake pastry shell according to package directions for making a filled pie.

2. In a large bowl, whisk together coconut milk, cooled coffee, sugar, and rum extract. Sprinkle dry pudding mix over coconut milk mixture; whisk for 2 minutes more. Gently fold in the 1 cup coconut and half of the whipped topping. Pour into baked and cooled pastry shell. Chill in refrigerator for at least 3 hours.

3. To serve, top pie with the remaining whipped topping and the ¼ cup toasted coconut.

*Note: Purchase one 6-serving-size package and one 4-serving-size package instant vanilla pudding and pie filling mix; measure out 1 cup of the dry mix to use in this recipe.

Strawberry-Kiwi Chiffon Pie

Prep 20 minutes   **Chill** 3 hours   **Makes** 8 servings

⅔   cup kiwi-strawberry soda, *Hansen's®*

1   package (8-serving-size) sugar-free low-calorie strawberry-kiwi gelatin, *Jell-O®*

½   cup cold water

2   ice cubes

1   tablespoon lime juice, *ReaLime®*

1   container (8 ounces) frozen whipped dessert topping, thawed, *Cool Whip®*

¾   cup chopped fresh strawberries

¾   cup chopped, peeled fresh kiwifruit

1   (6 ounces) shortbread pie crust, *Keebler® Ready Crust®*

     Kiwifruit slices

     Strawberry fan

1. In a large microwave-safe bowl, microwave soda on high about 2½ minutes or until boiling.

2. Add gelatin to hot soda, whisking until dissolved. Add cold water, ice cubes, and lime juice, stirring until mixture begins to thicken. Add whipped topping, whisking until combined. Gently fold in chopped strawberries and chopped kiwifruit.

3. Spoon mixture into shortbread crust. Chill in refrigerator about 3 hours or until set. Garnish with kiwifruit slices and strawberry fan.

Caramel-Banana Tart

Prep 30 minutes   **Bake** 10 minutes   **Cool** 1 hour   **Chill** 2 hours   **Oven** 450°F   **Makes** 1 (9-inch) tart

CRUST

½   **package (11 ounces) pie crust mix,** *Betty Crocker*®

¼   **cup orange juice**

FILLING

2   **cups milk**

1   **cup butterscotch caramel topping,** *Mrs. Richardson's*®

1   **package (4.4 ounces) custard dessert mix,** *Jell-O*®

1   **teaspoon imitation banana extract,** *McCormick*®

2   **large bananas**

1   **teaspoon rum extract,** *McCormick*®

1. Preheat oven to 450°F. In a medium bowl, combine pie crust mix and the ¼ cup orange juice, stirring until dough comes together. (If needed, add more juice, 1 teaspoon at a time.) Roll into a ball; turn out onto a lightly floured surface. Roll dough into a 10-inch-diameter circle. Fit dough circle into a 9-inch tart pan with a removable bottom. Prick the bottom of the crust with a fork.

2. Bake for 10 to 12 minutes or until golden brown. Cool in pan on a wire rack.

3. For filling, in a medium saucepan, combine milk, ½ cup of the caramel topping, and custard mix. Cook and stir over medium-high heat until boiling. Remove from heat; stir in banana extract. Cool for 15 minutes. Stir; cool for 15 minutes more.

4. Meanwhile, peel and cut both bananas in half. Cut each half in 3 lengthwise slices. In a medium skillet, combine the remaining ½ cup caramel topping and the rum extract; cook over medium-high heat until boiling, stirring occasionally. Add banana slices; boil for 1 minute. (Do not stir bananas and caramel, only shake the pan.) Using a metal spatula, carefully turn over bananas; boil for 1 minute more.

5. Using the spatula, transfer bananas to the cooled crust. Stir any caramel remaining in skillet into custard mixture. Pour custard mixture over bananas in tart shell. Chill in the refrigerator for at least 2 hours or until custard mixture sets up.

Peanut Tart
with Snickerdoodle Crust

Prep 30 minutes   **Bake** 35 minutes   **Oven** 375°F   **Makes** 1 (9-inch) tart

Nonstick cooking spray

1   pouch (17.3 ounces) sugar cookie mix, *Betty Crocker*®

1   tablespoon ground cinnamon, *McCormick*®

¼   teaspoon cream of tartar, *McCormick*®

¼   teaspoon ground cardamom, *Spice Islands*®

½   cup (1 stick) plus 1 tablespoon butter, melted

⅓   cup butterscotch chips, *Nestlé*®

1   cup roasted unsalted peanuts, *Planters*®

1   egg

⅓   cup light-color corn syrup, *Karo*®

¼   cup packed brown sugar, *Domino*®/*C&H*®

1. Preheat oven to 375°F. Spray a 9-inch tart pan with removable bottom with cooking spray; set aside. Line a baking sheet with foil; set aside.

2. In a large bowl, whisk together sugar cookie mix, cinnamon, cream of tartar, and cardamom. Add the ½ cup melted butter, stirring until mixture comes together. Press into bottom and up side of prepared tart pan. Sprinkle butterscotch chips and peanuts over cookie crust; set aside.

3. In a large bowl, whisk together egg, corn syrup, brown sugar, and the remaining 1 tablespoon butter. Pour mixture over chips and nuts in cookie crust. Place tart pan on prepared baking sheet.

4. Bake for 35 to 40 minutes or until set in center. Cool in pan on a wire rack. Remove tart from pan before slicing to serve.

Peanut Tart with Snickerdoodle

White Chocolate-Orange Chessman Cheesecake

Prep 40 minutes   **Bake** 1 hour   **Cool** 2 hours   **Oven** 350°F   **Makes** 8 servings

Nonstick cooking spray

2   cups plus 13 to 14 butter cookies, *Pepperidge Farm® Chessmen®*

3   tablespoons butter, melted

2   packages (8 ounces each) cream cheese, softened, *Philadelphia®*

1   package (4-serving-size) instant white chocolate pudding and pie filling mix, *Jell-O®*

¼   cup sugar, *Domino®/C&H®*

3   eggs

¼   cup sour cream

1¼   cups white baking chips, *Ghirardelli®*

½   cup heavy cream

½   cup frozen orange juice concentrate, thawed, *Minute Maid®*

White chocolate baking bar, shaved, *Ghirardelli®*

1. Preheat oven to 350°F. Spray an 8½- or 9-inch springform pan with cooking spray. Arrange 13 to 14 *Chessmen®* cookies, facing outward, around side of pan. (Cut more to fit if necessary.)

2. Place the 2 cups cookies in a large zip-top plastic bag. Press out air; seal bag. Using a rolling pin, crush cookies. Set aside 2 tablespoons of the crumbs. In a medium bowl, stir together the remaining cookie crumbs and melted butter until mixture comes together. Press into bottom and up the side of the cookie-lined pan; set aside.

3. In a large mixing bowl, beat cream cheese, pudding mix, and sugar with an electric mixer on medium until smooth. Add eggs, 1 at a time, beating well after each addition. Add sour cream; beat until combined. Pour into prepared cookie crust.

4. Place springform pan in a roasting pan; fill roasting pan with warm water to reach 1 inch up the side of the springform pan.

5. Bake for 60 to 65 minutes or until set in center. Remove springform pan from roasting pan; cool in springform pan on a wire rack.

6. For ganache, place white baking chips in a medium bowl. In a small saucepan, heat heavy cream and orange juice concentrate over medium heat just until boiling. Pour cream mixture over white baking chips, stirring with a rubber spatula until smooth. Let stand at room temperature until mixture thickens.

7. Remove cheesecake from springform pan; place on serving plate. Pour ganache on top of cake, but not over the side or the *Chessmen®* cookies. Garnish with white chocolate shavings. Sprinkle reserved cookie crumbs around the edge of the cheesecake and on top of the white chocolate shavings.

Snickerdoodle Cheesecake
with Caramel Sauce

Prep 30 minutes   **Bake** 40 minutes   **Cool** 2 hours   **Chill** 2 hours   **Oven** 350°F   **Makes** 10 servings

Nonstick cooking spray

1   **package (21 ounces) snickerdoodle cookie mix with spice packet,** *Krusteaz®*

½   **cup (1 stick) butter, melted**

2   **packages (8 ounces each) cream cheese, softened,** *Philadelphia®*

¼   **cup packed brown sugar,** *Domino®/C&H®*

3   **eggs**

¾   **cup caramel topping,** *Smucker's®*

¾   **teaspoon cinnamon extract,** *McCormick®*

1. Preheat oven to 350°F. Spray a 9-inch springform pan with cooking spray; set aside.

2. In a large bowl, combine snickerdoodle cookie mix, half of the spice packet from the cookie mix, and the butter, stirring until mixture comes together. Press mixture into bottom and up side of the prepared springform pan; set aside.

3. In a large mixing bowl, combine cream cheese, brown sugar, and the remaining spice from packet; beat with an electric mixer on medium until smooth. Add eggs, 1 at a time, beating well after each addition. Pour into cookie crust.

4. Bake for 40 to 45 minutes or until set with a soft-looking center. Cool in pan on a wire rack.

5. Meanwhile, in a small saucepan, heat caramel topping over medium-high heat until boiling; reduce heat to medium-low. Simmer about 5 minutes or until mixture thickens. Remove from heat; stir in cinnamon extract. Cool to room temperature.

6. Cut cooled cheesecake in wedges. Pour cooled caramel mixture over cheesecake. Chill in refrigerator for at least 2 hours before serving.

Chocolate-Dipped Strawberry Cheesecake

Prep 45 minutes   **Bake** 55 minutes   **Cool** 2 hours   **Chill** 20 minutes   **Oven** 350°F   **Makes** 8 servings

Nonstick cooking spray

2½   **cups chocolate-flavor graham cracker pieces, *Honey Maid® Sticks***

¼   **cup plus 1 tablespoon sugar, *Domino®/C&H®***

1   **tablespoon unsweetened cocoa powder, *Hershey's®***

¼   **cup (½ stick) butter, melted**

2   **packages (8 ounces each) cream cheese, softened, *Philadelphia®***

¼   **cup strawberry preserves, *Smucker's®***

3   **tablespoons instant cheesecake pudding and pie filling mix, *Jell-O®***

2   **teaspoons imitation strawberry extract, *McCormick®***

3   **eggs**

¼   **cup sour cream**

1   **container (7 ounces) dipping chocolate, *Baker's®***

10   **to 12 fresh whole strawberries, hulled**

1   **cup strawberry-flavor frozen whipped dessert topping, thawed, *Cool Whip®***

1. Preheat oven to 350°F. Spray an 8½- or 9-inch springform pan with cooking spray; set aside. Line a baking sheet with parchment paper; set aside.

2. In a food processor, combine graham crackers, the 1 tablespoon sugar, and the cocoa powder; cover and process until mixture forms fine crumbs. Add butter; pulse until mixture comes together. Press mixture into bottom of the prepared pan.

3. In a large mixing bowl, combine cream cheese, the remaining ¼ cup sugar, the preserves, pudding mix, and strawberry extract; beat with an electric mixer on medium until smooth. Add eggs, 1 at a time, beating well after each addition. Add sour cream; beat until combined. Pour into prepared crust. Place springform pan in roasting pan; fill roasting pan with warm water to reach 1 inch up the side of the springform pan. Bake for 55 to 60 minutes or until set in center. Cool in pan on a wire rack.

4. Meanwhile, microwave dipping chocolate in container on medium about 2 minutes or until completely melted, stirring every 30 seconds. Dip each strawberry into chocolate, coating half the berry. Place upright on prepared baking sheet. Chill in refrigerator about 20 minutes or until chocolate hardens.

5. To serve, remove cheesecake from the pan and place on serving plate. Place whipped topping dip in a small zip-top plastic bag. Press out air; seal bag. Snip off a small corner of the bag. Pipe whipped topping into 10 to 12 mounds on top of cheesecake. Top each mound with a chocolate-dipped strawberry. Serve immediately or chill in the refrigerator up to 4 hours.

American Fair

Some goodies appear at bake sales and potlucks all across America. Put any of these traditional treats on the table, and they'll disappear in a flash.

Apple-Cranberry Crumble
with Cheddar Cheese

Prep 20 minutes   **Bake** 45 minutes   **Oven** 450°F/375°F   **Makes** 6 servings

Nonstick cooking spray

2   cans (21 ounces each) apple pie filling, *Comstock®* or *Wilderness®*

²⁄₃ cup sweetened dried cranberries, *Craisins®*

¹⁄₄ cup sugar, *Domino®/C&H®*

3   tablespoons cornstarch

3   tablespoons cranberry juice, *Ocean Spray®*

2   cups pie crust mix, *Krusteaz®*

³⁄₄ cup shredded cheddar cheese, *Sargento® Classic ChefStyle*

¹⁄₂ cup chopped walnuts, *Planters®*

6   tablespoons packed brown sugar, *Domino®/C&H®*

¹⁄₃ cup cold butter, cut into pieces

Vanilla bean ice cream

1. Preheat oven to 450°F. Spray a 9-inch square baking pan with cooking spray; set aside.

2. In a large bowl, stir together apple pie filling, cranberries, and sugar. In a small bowl, combine cornstarch and cranberry juice, stirring until cornstarch is dissolved. Stir cornstarch mixture into fruit mixture until combined.

3. Spoon fruit-cornstarch mixture into the baking pan. For topping, in a medium bowl, stir together pie crust mix, cheese, walnuts, and brown sugar. Using a pastry blender or your hands, cut in butter until mixture resembles coarse crumbs. Sprinkle topping over fruit.

4. Bake for 15 minutes. Reduce oven temperature to 375°F. Bake for 30 to 40 minutes more or until topping is golden and fruit is bubbling. Serve warm with vanilla bean ice cream.

$3 50

Rhubarb-Strawberry Shortcake

Prep 20 minutes   **Bake** 10 minutes   **Cool** 1 hour   **Oven** 425°F   **Makes** 6 servings

RHUBARB-STRAWBERRY TOPPING

3   cups frozen rhubarb, thawed, *Dole*®

1   cup frozen sweetened sliced strawberries, thawed, *Dole*®

2   tablespoons sugar, *Domino*®/*C&H*®

1   tablespoon frozen orange juice concentrate, thawed, *Minute Maid*®

SHORTCAKES

2⅓   cups baking mix, *Bisquick*®

½   cup strawberry nectar, *Kern's*®

3   tablespoons sugar, *Domino*®/*C&H*®

3   tablespoons butter, melted

TOPPER

1   teaspoon imitation strawberry extract, *McCormick*®

2   drops red food coloring, *McCormick*®

1   container (8 ounces) frozen whipped dessert topping, thawed, *Cool Whip*®

1. For rhubarb-strawberry topping, in a large bowl, stir together rhubarb, sliced strawberries, the 2 tablespoons sugar, and the orange juice concentrate. Chill in refrigerator until ready to use.

2. For shortcakes, preheat oven to 425°F. In a large bowl, stir together baking mix, strawberry nectar, the 3 tablespoons sugar, and the melted butter until mixture forms a soft dough. Drop dough by 6 even spoonfuls onto an ungreased baking sheet. Bake for 10 to 12 minutes or until golden brown. Transfer shortcakes to a wire rack; cool completely.

3. For topper, add strawberry extract and red food coloring to whipped topping, stirring until combined.

4. To serve, split each cooled shortcake in half horizontally. Place shortcake bottoms on serving plates. Spoon rhubarb-strawberry topping over shortcake bottoms. Place shortcake tops on fruit. Spoon topper over.

Strawberry Mint Brownie Sundaes

Prep 30 minutes   **Bake** 35 minutes   **Cool** 1 hour   **Oven** 350°F   **Makes** 8 servings

1	pound fresh strawberries, sliced
¾	cup strawberry syrup, *Smucker's*®
	Nonstick cooking spray
1	package (18.3 ounces) fudge brownie mix, *Duncan Hines*®
⅔	cup vegetable oil
2	eggs
20	crème de menthe thins, unwrapped and chopped, *Andes*®
1	cup strawberry ice cream
1	cup mint chocolate chip ice cream
8	teaspoons chocolate syrup, *Hershey's*®
½	cup frozen whipped dessert topping, thawed, *Cool Whip*®
8	teaspoons nut topping, *Diamond of California*®

1. In a medium bowl, stir together sliced strawberries and ½ cup of the strawberry syrup. Chill in refrigerator until ready to serve.

2. Preheat oven to 350°F. Spray a 9-inch-square baking pan with cooking spray; set aside.

3. In a large bowl, stir together brownie mix, the oil, eggs, and the remaining ¼ cup strawberry syrup until well mixed. Stir in chopped crème de menthe thins. Pour into prepared pan.

4. Bake for 35 to 45 minutes or until set in center. Cool brownies in pan on a wire rack.

5. Cut brownies into 8 servings and place on serving plates.

6. For each serving, top a brownie with 3 tablespoons of the strawberry mixture. Top strawberries with a small scoop (about 2 tablespoons) of the strawberry ice cream and a small scoop of the mint chocolate chip ice cream (about 2 tablespoons). Pour a heaping teaspoonful of the chocolate syrup over the ice cream; top with a tablespoonful of the whipped topping. Sprinkle with a teaspoonful of the nut topping.

Rocky Road Parfaits

Prep 20 minutes   **Chill** 2 hours   **Makes** 8 servings

1   cup semisweet chocolate chips, *Nestlé*®

2   cups cold chocolate milk,* *Nesquik*®

1   package (3.4-ounce) instant chocolate pudding and pie filling mix,* *Jell-O*®

1   teaspoon almond extract, *McCormick*®

4   (4 ounces each) purchased chocolate chip muffins, cut into 1-inch pieces (4 cups total)

2   cups tiny marshmallows, *Kraft*® *Jet-Puffed*®

1   cup sliced almonds, *Planters*®

1. In a small microwave-safe bowl, microwave chocolate chips on medium about 2 minutes or until melted, stirring every 30 seconds.

2. In a large bowl, combine chocolate milk and dry pudding mix; whisk for 2 minutes. Let stand about 3 minutes or until thick. Stir in almond extract.

3. To serve, equally divide the ingredients in the following order in each of 8 dessert glasses: chocolate pudding, muffin pieces, marshmallows, melted chocolate, and almonds. Chill 2 hours.

4. Serve chilled or at room temperature.

*Note: For an ice cream treat, substitute 1 pint chocolate ice cream, softened, for the chocolate milk and pudding mix.

Carrot Cake Bread Pudding

Prep 15 minutes   **Bake** 35 minutes   **Oven** 350°F   **Makes** 6 servings

Nonstick cooking spray

1   package (17.5 ounces) frozen carrot cake, thawed and cut into 1-inch cubes,* *Mrs. Smith's*®

¾   cup chopped walnuts, *Planters*®

¼   cup golden raisins, *Sun-Maid*®

1¼   cups milk

1   package (4-serving-size) instant butterscotch pudding and pie filling mix, *Jell-O*®

½   teaspoon ground cinnamon, *McCormick*®

2   tablespoons butter, cut into pieces

Frozen whipped dessert topping, thawed, *Cool Whip*®

1. Preheat oven to 350°F. Spray a 2-quart casserole with cooking spray; set aside.

2. In a large mixing bowl, combine carrot cake cubes, walnuts, and raisins.

3. Combine milk, dry pudding mix, and cinnamon; whisk until well mixed. Pour over carrot cake mixture, stirring gently. Pour into prepared casserole. Dot with butter.

4. Bake for 35 to 45 minutes or until hot in center. Serve warm with whipped topping.

*Note: If you prefer, substitute leftover homemade carrot cake for the frozen cake. It's a great way use leftover cake, especially if the cake is a little dry.

Louisiana Mud Slide

Prep 25 minutes   **Freeze** 15 minutes + 1 hour + 4 hours   **Makes** 10 servings

½ **cup caramel topping,**
   Mrs. Richardson's®

2 **teaspoons vanilla extract,**
   McCormick®

1 **(9-inch) chocolate pie crust,**
   Keebler® *Ready Crust*®

2 **pints coffee ice cream, softened**
   separately

½ **cup semisweet chocolate chips,**
   Nestlé®

½ **cup finely chopped pecans,**
   Planters®

1. In a small saucepan, stir together caramel topping and vanilla extract. Cook and stir over medium heat just until boiling; reduce heat to low. Simmer for 8 minutes. Set aside to cool.

2. Spoon ¼ cup of the cooled caramel mixture into pie crust; freeze about 15 minutes or until caramel is firm. Remove pie crust from freezer. Using a rubber spatula, spread one pint of the softened ice cream over caramel. Sprinkle half the chocolate chips and half the pecans over the ice cream. Freeze for 1 hour more.

3. Remove pie from freezer. Spread the remaining pint softened ice cream into the pie. Sprinkle the remaining chocolate chips and the remaining pecans. Top with the remaining caramel mixture. Freeze at least 4 hours before serving.

Note: For easy serving, run a knife under hot water and wipe clean after each slice.

Red, White, and Blue Ice Cream Sandwiches

Prep 45 minutes   **Bake** 15 minutes   **Cool** 1 hour   **Freeze** 1 hour   **Oven** 350°F
Makes 9 round and 9 star ice cream sandwiches

1   package (18.25 ounces) vanilla cake mix, *Duncan Hines*®

⅓   cup vegetable oil

2   eggs

4   teaspoons red food coloring, *McCormick*®

2   teaspoons blue food coloring, *McCormick*®

1   carton (1.75 quarts) vanilla bean ice cream, softened

1   cup red sprinkles, *Betty Crocker*®

1   cup blue sprinkles, *Betty Crocker*®

1. Preheat oven to 350°F. Line two 9-inch-square baking pans with parchment paper; set aside.

2. In a large mixing bowl, combine cake mix, oil, and eggs; beat with an electric mixer on low for 30 seconds. Scrape down side of bowl; beat on medium for 1 minute. Batter will be thick. Pour half of the batter into a medium bowl; stir in red food coloring until well mixed. Stir blue food coloring into the other half of batter. Spread red batter into one of the prepared pans and blue batter into the other prepared pan.

3. Bake both pans for 15 to 18 minutes or until a toothpick inserted in centers comes out clean, rotating pans once halfway through baking. Cool in pans on a wire rack for 30 minutes. Remove from pans; cool completely on rack.

4. Thoroughly wash baking pans; dry completely. Divide softened ice cream between the clean 9-inch-square pans, spreading evenly to about ½-inch thickness. Cover with plastic wrap. Freeze for 1 hour.

5. Using a 3-inch round cookie cutter, cut 9 circles from the red cake and 9 circles from the blue cake. Using a 1-inch star cookie cutter, cut a star shape from center of each cake circle. Carefully remove stars from centers of the cake circles; set aside. Using the round cookie cutter, cut 9 circles from the ice cream in pans; using the star cutter, cut 9 stars from the ice cream. Refreeze if necessary.

6. Pour colored sprinkles into separate rimmed dishes.

7. To assemble, using a wide metal spatula, carefully place an ice cream circle on one of the blue cake circles; top with a red cake circle. Roll edge in colored sprinkles. Repeat to make 9 round sandwiches total. Repeat with star-shape ice cream and cake. Serve immediately or wrap individually with plastic wrap and freeze.

$1^{50}

Black and White Refrigerator Cake

Prep 35 minutes   **Chill** 4 hours   **Makes** 8 servings

Nonstick cooking spray

2 cups graham cracker crumbs, *Honey Maid®*

6 tablespoons sugar, *Domino®/C&H®*

6 tablespoons butter, melted

3 tablespoons unsweetened cocoa powder, *Hershey's®*

2 packages (8 ounces each) cream cheese, softened, *Philadelphia®*

1 jar (7 ounces) marshmallow creme, *Kraft®*

1 cup heavy cream

3 tablespoons instant cheesecake pudding and pie filling mix, *Jell-O®*

1¼ cups semisweet chocolate chips, *Nestlé®*

1 container (8 ounces) frozen whipped dessert topping, thawed, *Cool Whip® Extra Creamy*

Frozen whipped dessert topping, thawed (optional), *Cool Whip®*

1. Spray an 8½-inch springform pan with cooking spray; set aside.

2. In a medium bowl, using a fork, stir together 1 cup of the graham cracker crumbs, 2 tablespoons of the sugar, and 3 tablespoons of the melted butter until the mixture comes together. Press mixture into one half of the springform pan.

3. In a medium bowl, stir together the remaining 1 cup graham cracker crumbs, the remaining 4 tablespoons sugar, and the cocoa powder. Drizzle the remaining 3 tablespoons melted butter over; stir with a fork until mixture comes together. Press into the other half of the pan; set aside.

4. In a large mixing bowl, beat cream cheese and marshmallow creme with an electric mixer on medium until smooth; set aside.

5. In another large mixing bowl, combine heavy cream and dry pudding mix; beat with an electric mixer on medium to high until stiff peaks form. Add half the cream cheese mixture, stirring until smooth. Spread pudding mixture over the chocolate half of the crumb crust.

6. In a medium microwave-safe bowl, microwave chocolate chips on medium about 2 minutes or until melted, stirring every 30 seconds. Cool to room temperature. In a medium bowl, pour melted chocolate over the 8-ounce container whipped topping; stir until combined. Spread whipped topping mixture over plain half of the crumb crust.

7. Using a table knife, smooth the tops of both sides and the middle of the cake. Cover with plastic wrap. Chill in refrigerator for at least 4 hours. Remove cake from springform pan. If desired, top with additional whipped topping. Cut into wedges; serve immediately.

Sweet Potato and Pumpkin Pie

Prep 25 minutes   **Bake** 10 minutes + 1 hour   **Cool** 1 hour   Oven 375°F/325°F   **Makes** 8 servings

1   (9-inch) frozen unbaked deep-dish pastry shell, thawed, *Mrs. Smith's*®

PUMPKIN CREAM CHEESE LAYER

1   package (8 ounces) cream cheese, softened, *Philadelphia*®

¼   cup sugar, *Domino*®/*C&H*®

¼   cup canned solid-pack pumpkin, *Libby's*®

1   egg

1   teaspoon imitation maple flavoring, *McCormick*®

1   teaspoon pumpkin pie spice, *McCormick*®

SWEET POTATO LAYER

1   can (15 ounces) cut sweet potatoes, *Princella*®

2   teaspoons vanilla extract, *McCormick*®

1   can (14 ounces) sweetened condensed milk, *Eagle Brand*®

2   eggs

2   teaspoons ground cinnamon, *McCormick*®

1   teaspoon pumpkin pie spice, *McCormick*®

     Frozen whipped dessert topping, thawed (optional), *Cool Whip*®

1. Preheat oven to 375°F. Line a baking sheet with foil.

2. Prick the bottom of the pastry shell with a fork; place on prepared baking sheet. Bake for 10 to 12 minutes or until golden brown. Transfer to a wire rack; cool completely.

3. Reduce oven temperature to 325°F.

4. For pumpkin cream cheese layer, in a small mixing bowl, beat cream cheese and sugar with an electric mixer on medium until creamy. Add pumpkin, the 1 egg, the maple extract, and 1 teaspoon pumpkin pie spice; beat until smooth. Spoon cream cheese mixture into the cooled pastry shell. Spread mixture on the bottom and up the side of the pastry shell; set aside.

5. For sweet potato layer, in a large mixing bowl, beat sweet potatoes and vanilla extract with electric mixer on low until smooth. Add sweetened condensed milk, the 2 eggs, the cinnamon, and 1 teaspoon pumpkin pie spice; beat until smooth. Pour over cream cheese layer to fill pastry shell.

6. Bake for 1 to 1¼ hours or until set in center. Cool on a wire rack. Cover and chill within 2 hours. If desired, serve with whipped topping.

Sweet Potato
Pumpkin Pie
$6.⁰⁰

Cherry-Lemon Meringue Mini Pies

Prep 30 minutes   **Bake** 10 minutes   **Cool** 1 hour   **Chill** 2 hours   **Oven** 350°F   **Makes** 16 mini pies

MERINGUE CUPS

Nonstick cooking spray

2 containers (5 ounces each) vanilla meringue cookies (48 cookies), *Miss Meringue*®

¾ cup cake flour, *Swans Down*®

1 cup (2 sticks) butter, melted

LEMON FILLING

1 package (4-serving-size) cook-and-serve lemon pudding and pie filling mix, *Jell-O*®

½ cup sugar, *Domino*®/*C&H*®

2¼ cups lemonade, *Minute Maid*®

2 egg yolks

1 cup cherry pie filling, *Comstock*® or *Wilderness*®

Frozen whipped dessert topping, thawed (optional), *Cool Whip*®

1. For meringue cups, preheat oven to 350°F. Spray sixteen 2½-inch muffin cups with cooking spray; set aside.

2. In a food processor, combine meringue cookies and cake flour; cover and process until like fine crumbs. Add melted butter and pulse until well mixed. Spoon 1 tablespoon of the meringue mixture into each of the prepared muffin cups. Using the back of a measuring tablespoon, press mixture into bottoms and up sides of cups.

3. Bake for 10 to 12 minutes or just until starting to brown. Remove from oven. Immediately press each cup with the back of the measuring tablespoon. Cool in muffin cups on a wire rack.

4. For lemon filling, in a medium saucepan, combine lemon pudding mix and sugar. Whisk in lemonade and egg yolks. Cook and whisk over medium-high heat until mixture comes to a rolling boil. Remove from heat. Cool for 5 minutes.

5. Spoon 2 tablespoons of the lemon filling into each cooled meringue cup. (Reserve remaining lemon filling for another use.) Top each filled cup with 1 tablespoon of the cherry pie filling. Chill in refrigerator about 2 hours or until set.

6. Serve chilled or at room temperature. If desired, top each mini pie with a spoonful of whipped topping.

Cookiescapes

Whether you make one of these stunning arrangements as a gift, a centerpiece, or as a bake sale item to outshine all others, sheer fun is part of the process.

Couture Cookies

Prep 25 minutes   **Chill** 2 hours + 1 hour   **Bake** 8 minutes per batch   **Cool** 5 minutes per batch
Decorating 50 minutes   **Oven** 350°F   **Makes** 2 small, 10 medium, and 6 large cookies

CHERRY CHIP COOKIES

1   pouch (17.5 ounces) sugar cookie mix, *Betty Crocker*®

¼   cup dried cherries, finely chopped, *Sun-Maid*®

3   tablespoons all-purpose flour

⅓   cup butter, softened

1   egg

1   teaspoon imitation bubblegum extract, *McCormick*®

DECORATIONS

1   can (12 ounces) whipped whipped cream frosting, *Betty Crocker*®

Colored decorating icings, *Cake Mate*® *Easy Squeeze* or *Betty Crocker*® *Easy Flow*

Colored decorating gels, *Cake Mate*®

Colored sparkling sugar, sanding sugar, edible glitter, and/or dragées*

Small jelly beans, *Jelly Belly*®

This a fancy cookie assortment for a young girl's party with a fashion-design theme. Let party guests decorate their own cookies, using women's fashion magazines for inspiration.

1. For cookies, in a large bowl, combine sugar cookie mix, dried cherries, and flour. Add butter, egg, and bubblegum extract, stirring until mixture forms a dough. Shape dough into a ball; flatten into a disk. Wrap disk in plastic wrap. Chill in refrigerator for at least 2 hours.

2. Line cookie sheets with parchment paper; set aside. On a lightly floured surface, roll out chilled dough to ¼-inch thickness. Using clothing-shape cookie cutters, cut out shapes. Reroll scrap dough to cut out more shapes. Transfer same-size cookies to prepared cookie sheets, spacing cookies 2 inches apart.** Chill cutout cookies in refrigerator for at least 1 hour.

3. Preheat oven to 350°F. Bake cookies for 8 to 14 minutes (depending on size) or until cookies are puffed and tops look cracked. Cool on cookie sheets for 5 minutes. Transfer cookies to a wire rack; cool completely.

4. For icing, spoon frosting into a glass pie plate; microwave on high for 20 seconds. Dip one side of each cooled cookie into melted frosting; if necessary, smooth with the back of a spoon. Place cookies, frosting sides up, on wire rack; let stand until frosting hardens.

5. Decorate iced cookies as desired with various colored decorating icing, decorating gels, sugars, edible glitter, dragées, and/or jelly beans.

***Note:** Remove and discard dragées before eating cookies.

****Note:** Arrange same-size cookies together on cookie sheet so small shapes don't overbake while large shapes take longer to fully bake.

Couture Cookies
$16.00

Lilly Pond Picnic

Prep 30 minutes   **Chill** I hour + I hour   **Bake** 8 minutes per batch   **Cool** 5 minutes per batch
Decorating 45 minutes   **Oven** 350°F   **Makes** 10 small, 6 medium, and 2 large cookies

COOKIES

I   pouch (17.5 ounces) sugar cookie mix, *Betty Crocker®*

I   tablespoon all-purpose flour

⅓   cup butter, softened

I   egg

2   teaspoons almond extract, *McCormick®*

DECORATIONS

Sucker sticks

Florist's wire

Colored decorating icings, *Cake Mate® Easy Squeeze* or *Betty Crocker® Easy Flow*

Colored decorating gels, *Cake Mate®*

My house is called Lilly Pond—and there are all sorts of insects and bugs who call it their home too. They flutter and fly in like little fairies, landing on the lily pads that float on top of the pond.

I. For cookies, in a large bowl, combine sugar cookie mix and flour. Add butter, egg, and extract, stirring until mixture forms a dough. Shape dough into a ball; flatten into a disk. Wrap disk in plastic wrap. Chill in refrigerator for at least I hour.

2. Line cookie sheets with parchment paper; set aside. On a lightly floured surface, roll out chilled dough to ½-inch thickness. Using insect-shape cookie cutters, cut out various shapes. Reroll scrap dough to cut out more shapes. Transfer same-size cookies to prepared cookie sheets, spacing cookies 2 inches apart.* Carefully insert a sucker stick into each cookie, pressing firmly. Chill cutout cookies in refrigerator for at least I hour. (For bees, bake cookies first, then insert florist's wire after decorating.)

3. Preheat oven to 350°F. Bake cookies for 8 to 14 minutes (depending on size) or until cookies are puffed. Cool on cookie sheets for 5 minutes. Transfer cookies to a wire rack; cool completely.

4. Decorate cookies as desired with colored icings and decorating gels.

*Note: Arrange same-size cookies together on cookie sheet so small shapes don't overbake while waiting for larger shapes to fully bake.

Easy Easter Basket

Prep 25 minutes **Chill** 1 hour + 1 hour **Bake** 15 minutes per batch **Cool** 5 minutes per batch
Decorating 45 minutes **Oven** 350°F **Makes** 12 large cookies

COOKIES

1	tube (16.5 ounces) refrigerated sugar cookie dough, *Pillsbury*®
1¼	cups all-purpose flour
½	teaspoon cherry flavoring
12	sucker sticks

DECORATIONS

Colored decorating icings, *Cake Mate*® *Easy Squeeze* or *Betty Crocker*® *Easy Flow*

Tiny colored candies

Colored decorating gels, *Cake Mate*®

Colored sparkling sugar, *India Tree*®

Colored sanding sugar

This makes a charming centerpiece for Easter dinner—and when the last bit of ham and scalloped potatoes is gone, it makes a tasty dessert as well. Secure the sticks in florist's foam for stability.

1. For cookies, in a large bowl, stir together cookie dough, flour, and cherry flavoring until well mixed. Shape dough into a ball; flatten into a disk. Wrap disk in plastic wrap. Chill in refrigerator for at least 1 hour.

2. Line cookie sheets with parchment paper; set aside. On a lightly floured surface, roll out chilled dough to ½-inch thickness. Using Easter-shape cookie cutters, cut out various shapes. Reroll scrap dough to cut out more shapes. Transfer same-size cookies to prepared cookie sheets, spacing cookies 2 inches apart.* Carefully insert a sucker stick into each cookie, pressing firmly. Chill cutout cookies in refrigerator for at least 1 hour.

3. Preheat oven to 350°F. Bake cookies for 15 to 18 minutes (depending on size) or until cookies are puffed. Cool on cookie sheets for 5 minutes. Transfer cookies to a wire rack; cool completely.

4. Decorate cooled cookies as desired with colored icings, tiny colored candies, decorating gels, and/or colored sugars.

*Note: Arrange same-size cookies together on cookie sheet so small shapes don't overbake while large shapes take longer to fully bake.

Safari Soiree

Prep 55 minutes   **Chill** I hour + I hour   **Bake** 10 minutes per batch   **Cool** 5 minutes per batch
Decorating I hour   **Oven** 350°F   **Makes** 56 medium and 2 large cookies

BLACK AND WHITE COOKIES

I	pouch (17.5 ounces) sugar cookie mix, *Betty Crocker*®
3	tablespoons all-purpose flour
1/3	cup butter, softened
3	tablespoons refrigerated liquid egg whites, *All Whites*®
1/4	teaspoon imitation maple extract, *McCormick*®
2	drops black food coloring, *McCormick*®

YELLOW AND BROWN COOKIES

I	package (18 ounces) ready-to-bake refrigerated sugar cookie dough, *Pillsbury*® *Ready to Bake*®
I	tablespoon all-purpose flour
1/2	teaspoon imitation banana extract, *McCormick*®
3	drops yellow food coloring, *McCormick*®
I	tablespoon unsweetened cocoa powder, *Hershey's*®

DECORATIONS

I	can (12 ounces) whipped chocolate frosting, *Duncan Hines*®
	Chocolate bar, grated, *Hershey's*®
	Colored sanding sugar
	Colored decorating icings, *Cake Mate*® *Easy Squeeze* or *Betty Crocker*® *Easy Flow*
	Colored sparkling sugar, *India Tree*®
	Candy-coated sunflower seeds

Whimsical zoo creatures peer out at party guests from a wooden bowl filled with peanuts. For a safari-theme children's party—or after a visit to the zoo—send them home with guests as favors.

I. Line cookie sheets with parchment paper; set aside. For black and white cookies, in a large bowl, combine cookie mix, 2 tablespoons of the flour, the butter, and egg whites, stirring until a dough forms. Shape three-fourths of the dough into a disk. Add remaining I tablespoon flour, maple extract, and black food coloring to the remaining dough in bowl, stirring until well mixed. Shape into a disk. Wrap disks in plastic wrap. Chill in refrigerator for I hour.

2. On a lightly floured surface, roll out some chilled white dough to ½-inch thickness. Pinch off a piece of black dough; divide into several pieces and roll each piece into a thin rope. Place each black rope at an angle on the white dough; roll over to flatten into white dough. Using a zebra-shape cookie cutter, cut out shapes. Reroll scrap dough and cut out more zebra shapes. Roll out remaining white dough to ½-inch thickness; cut with elephant- and/ or lion-shape cookie cutters. Reroll scrap dough and cut out more shapes.

3. Transfer same-size cookies to prepared cookie sheets, spacing cookies 2 inches apart.* Chill cutout cookies in refrigerator for at least I hour.

4. Preheat oven to 350°F. Bake cookies for I0 to I2 minutes (depending on size) or until cookies are puffed and tops look cracked. Cool on cookie sheets for 5 minutes. Transfer cookies to a wire rack; cool completely.

5. For yellow and brown cookies, divide ready-to-bake cookie dough in half. Place each half in a medium bowl. Add I tablespoon flour, banana extract, and yellow food coloring to half the dough; stir until well mixed. Shape yellow dough into a disk. Add the cocoa powder to the remaining cookie dough, stirring until well mixed. Shape into a disk. Wrap disks in plastic. Chill in refrigerator for I hour.

6. On a lightly floured surface, roll out chilled yellow dough to ½-inch thickness. Pinch off small pieces of the brown dough; press into yellow dough and roll over to flatten into yellow dough. Using a giraffe-shape cookie cutter, cut out shapes. Reroll yellow scrap dough with more brown for a marble effect; use elephant- or lion-shape cookie cutters to cut into shapes. Roll any remaining brown dough to ¼-inch thickness; use a monkey-shape cookie cutter to cut shapes.

7. Continue as directed in Steps 3 and 4 above.

8. Decorate cookies as desired with colored decorating icing, sparkling sugar, and candy-coated sunflower seeds.

***Note:** Arrange same-size cookies together on cookie sheet so small shapes don't overbake while large shapes take longer to fully bake.

Patriotic Parade

Prep 50 minutes   **Chill** 2 hours + 1 hour   **Bake** 6 minutes per batch   **Cool** 5 minutes per batch
Decorating 1¼ hours   **Oven** 350°F   **Makes** 48 small, 24 medium, and 6 large cookies

RED COOKIES

- 1   pouch (17.5 ounces) sugar cookie mix, *Betty Crocker*®
- 1   tablespoon all-purpose flour
- ⅓   cup butter, softened
- 1   egg
- 2   teaspoons imitation raspberry extract, *McCormick*®
- 8   drops red food coloring, *McCormick*®

  Sucker sticks

WHITE COOKIES

- 1   pouch (17.5 ounces) sugar cookie mix, *Betty Crocker*®
- 1   tablespoon all-purpose flour
- ⅓   cup butter, softened
- 1   egg
- 2   teaspoons vanilla extract, *McCormick*®

BLUE COOKIES

- 1   tube (16.5 ounces) refrigerated sugar cookie dough, *Pillsbury*®
- ½   cup all-purpose flour
- 2   tablespoons blueberry syrup, *Smucker's*®

DECORATIONS

- 1   can (12 ounces) whipped fluffy white frosting (optional), *Duncan Hines*®

  Red, white, and blue decorating icings and gels

  Red, white, and blue sparkling sugar, sanding sugar, sprinkles, and/or star candies

Add sparkle to the table at a Fourth of July picnic with these treats. Play old-fashioned games—such as sack races, water-balloon toss, and egg-spoon relay races—and hand these out to the winners.

1. For red cookies, in a large bowl, combine 1 pouch sugar cookie mix and 1 tablespoon flour. Add ⅓ cup butter, 1 egg, the raspberry extract, and red food coloring, stirring until mixture forms a dough. Shape dough into a ball; flatten into a disk. Wrap disk in plastic wrap. Chill in refrigerator for at least 2 hours.

2. Line cookie sheets with parchment paper; set aside. On a lightly floured surface, roll out chilled dough to ½-inch thickness. Using Independence Day-theme cookie cutters, cut out various shapes. Reroll scrap dough to cut out more shapes. Transfer same-size cookies to prepared cookie sheets, spacing cookies 2 inches apart.* Carefully insert a sucker stick into each cookie, pressing firmly. Chill cutout cookies in refrigerator for at least 1 hour.

3. Preheat oven to 350°F. Bake cookies for 6 to 12 minutes (depending on size) or until cookies are puffed. Cool on cookie sheets for 5 minutes. Transfer cookies to a wire rack; cool completely.

4. For white cookies, in a large bowl, combine 1 pouch sugar cookie mix and 1 tablespoon flour. Add ⅓ cup butter, 1 egg, and the vanilla extract, stirring until mixture forms a dough. Shape dough into a ball; flatten into a disk. Wrap disk in plastic wrap. Chill in refrigerator for at least 2 hours.

5. Continue as directed in Steps 2 and 3 above.

6. For blue cookies, in a large bowl, stir together sugar cookie dough, the ½ cup flour, and the blueberry syrup until well mixed. Shape dough into a ball; flatten into a disk. Wrap disk in plastic wrap. Chill in refrigerator for at least 2 hours.

7. Continue as directed in Steps 2 and 3 above.

8. To decorate cookies, spread fluffy white frosting on cooled cookies. Decorate with decorating icings and gels, sparkling sugar, sanding sugar, sprinkles, and/or star candies.

*Note: Arrange same-size cookies together on cookie sheet so small shapes don't overbake while large shapes take longer to fully bake.

Barking Bash

Prep 30 minutes   **Chill** 30 minutes + 1 hour   **Bake** 8 minutes per batch   **Cool** 5 minutes per batch
Decorating 35 minutes   **Oven** 350°F   **Makes** 6 small, 20 medium, and 6 large cookies

COOKIES

1   pouch (17.5 ounces) sugar cookie mix, *Betty Crocker*®

2   tablespoons packed dark brown sugar, *C&H*®

1   tablespoon all-purpose flour

1½ teaspoons ground cinnamon, *McCormick*®

⅓   cup butter, softened

1   egg

DECORATIONS

2   cans (12 ounces each) whipped buttercream frosting, *Betty Crocker*®

    Red food coloring, *McCormick*®

    Chocolate bar, grated, *Hershey's*®

    White chocolate bar, grated, *Ghirardelli*®

    Colored sanding sugar

    Colored sparkling sugar, *India Tree*®

    Colored decorating icings, *Cake Mate*® *Easy Squeeze* or *Betty Crocker*® *Easy Flow*

These cookies are for people to eat—not for dogs! Host a "puppy shower" for a friend who has just adopted a canine family member and make these as "people treats" for human guests.

1. For cookies, in a large bowl, combine sugar cookie mix, brown sugar, flour, and cinnamon. Add butter and egg, stirring until mixture forms a dough. Shape dough into a ball; flatten into a disk. Wrap disk in plastic wrap. Chill in refrigerator for at least 30 minutes.

2. Line cookie sheets with parchment paper; set aside. On a lightly floured surface, roll out chilled dough to ¼-inch thickness. Using dog-shape or bone-shape cookie cutters, cut out shapes. Reroll scrap dough to cut out more shapes. Transfer same-size cookies to prepared cookie sheets, spacing cookies 2 inches apart.* Chill cutout cookies in refrigerator for at least 1 hour.

3. Preheat oven to 350°F. Bake cookies for 8 to 15 minutes (depending on size) or until cookies are puffed. Cool on cookie sheets for 5 minutes. Transfer cookies to a wire rack; cool completely.

4. To decorate cookies, tint one of the containers of frosting with red food coloring. Frost a cookie with red or plain frosting. For fur, sprinkle frosting with grated chocolate, grated white chocolate, or sanding sugar. Decorate other cooled cookies as desired with frosting, sanding sugar, sparkling sugar, and/or colored decorating icing.

*Note: Arrange same-size cookies together on cookie sheet so small shapes don't overbake while large shapes take longer to fully bake.

Haute Halloween

Prep 45 minutes   **Chill** 1 hour + 1 hour   **Bake** 8 minutes per batch; 13 minutes per batch   **Cool** 5 minutes per batch
Decorating 1 hour   **Oven** 350°F/375°F   **Makes** 12 small, 16 medium, and 12 large cookies

CHOCOLATE COOKIES

1   pouch (17.5 ounces) double chocolate chunk cookie mix, *Betty Crocker®*

¼   cup all-purpose flour

6   tablespoons butter, softened

1   egg

Wooden sucker sticks

CHOCOLATE CHUNK COOKIES

1   pouch (17.5 ounces) double chocolate chunk cookie mix, *Betty Crocker®*

¼   cup all-purpose flour

6   tablespoons butter, softened

1   egg

Sucker sticks

DECORATIONS

Colored sanding sugar

Nonpareil sprinkles

Chocolate bar, grated, *Hershey's®*

White chocolate baking bar, grated

Colored decorating icings, *Cake Mate® Easy Squeeze* or *Betty Crocker® Easy Flow*

Powdered sugar, *Domino®/C&H®*

More smile-inducing than spooky, these whimsical suckers tucked into a rustic copper "cauldron" make a perfect centerpiece for a Halloween party. Send them home with guests as treats.

1. For chocolate cookies, spoon 1 pouch chocolate chunk cookie mix into a wire-mesh strainer set over a large bowl. Sift cookie mix through strainer, leaving chocolate chunks in strainer (reserve chocolate chunks to use for decorating cookies). Stir ¼ cup flour into cookie mix in bowl. Add 6 tablespoons butter and 1 egg; stir until mixture forms a dough. Shape dough into a ball; flatten into a disk. Wrap disk in plastic wrap. Chill in refrigerator for at least 1 hour.

2. Line cookie sheets with parchment paper; set aside. On a lightly floured surface, roll out chilled dough to ½-inch thickness. Using Halloween cookie cutters, cut out shapes. Reroll scrap dough to cut out more shapes. Transfer same-size cookies to prepared cookie sheets, spacing cookies 2 inches apart.* Carefully insert a sucker stick into each cookie, pressing firmly. Chill cutout cookies in refrigerator for at least 1 hour.

3. Preheat oven to 350°F. Bake cookies for 8 to 12 minutes (depending on size) or until cookies are puffed. Cool on cookie sheets for 5 minutes. Transfer cookies to a wire rack; cool completely.

4. For chocolate chunk cookies, preheat oven to 375°F. Line cookie sheets with parchment paper; set aside.

5. In a large bowl, combine 1 pouch chocolate chunk cookie mix and ¼ cup flour. Add 6 tablespoons butter and 1 egg; stir until mixture forms a dough. For a cookie template, place a Halloween cookie cutter on prepared cookie sheet. Press a scoop of the chocolate chunk cookie dough into cutter to make shape. Lift off cookie cutter. Repeat with the remaining chocolate chunk cookie dough, spacing shapes 2 inches apart. Carefully insert a sucker stick into each cookie, pressing firmly.

6. Bake for 13 to 17 minutes or just until set in centers. Cool on cookie sheets for 5 minutes. Transfer cookies to a wire rack; cool completely.

7. Place reserved chocolate chunks (from cookie mix in Step 1) in a small microwave-safe bowl; microwave on medium about 2 minutes or until melted, stirring every 30 seconds. Spread melted chocolate on some of the cookies; sprinkle with sanding sugar, sprinkles, or grated chocolate to resemble cat or bat fur.

8. Decorate remaining cooled cookies as desired with decorating icings, sanding sugar, sprinkles, and/or powdered sugar.

*Note: Arrange same-size cookies together on cookie sheet so small shapes don't overbake while large shapes take longer to fully bake.

$4.00

An Ocean Spray

Prep 30 minutes   **Chill** 1 hour + 1 hour   **Bake** 10 minutes per batch   **Cool** 5 minutes per batch
Decorating 50 minutes   **Oven** 350°F   **Makes** 14 medium and 8 large cookies

COOKIES

1   pouch (17.5 ounces) sugar cookie mix, *Betty Crocker*®

2   tablespoons all-purpose flour

⅓   cup butter, softened

1   egg

1   tablespoon frozen lemon juice, thawed, *Minute Maid*®

DECORATIONS

Colored decorating icings, *Cake Mate*® *Easy Squeeze* or *Betty Crocker*® *Easy Flow*

Colored decorating gels, *Cake Mate*®

Colored sparkling sugar, *India Tree*®

Colored sanding sugar

Pull-apart twist candy, *Twizzlers*® *Pull-n-Peel*

Fruit leather

Chocolate-covered malted milk balls

Tiny candy-coated chocolate pieces, *M&M's*® *Minis*

When you need a bit of beach attitude in your latitude, put together this breezy cookie collection for a summer party or luau. Nestle the cookies into a tray full of brown sugar "sand."

1. For cookies, in a large bowl, combine sugar cookie mix and flour. Add butter, egg, and lemon juice, stirring until mixture forms a dough. Shape dough into a ball; flatten into a disk. Wrap disk in plastic wrap. Chill in refrigerator for at least 1 hour.

2. Line cookie sheets with parchment paper; set aside. On a lightly floured surface, roll out chilled dough to ¼-inch thickness. Using beach-theme cookie cutters, cut out various shapes. Reroll scrap dough to cut out more shapes. Transfer same-size cookies to prepared cookie sheets, spacing cookies 2 inches apart.* Chill cutout cookies in refrigerator for at least 1 hour.

3. Preheat oven to 350°F. Bake cookies for 10 to 14 minutes (depending on size) or until cookies are puffed. Cool on cookie sheets for 5 minutes. Transfer cookies to a wire rack; cool completely.

4. Decorate cooled cookies with colored decorating icings, decorating gels, sugars, strips of twist candy, fruit leather, and/or candy-coated chocolate pieces.

*Note: Arrange same-size cookies together on cookie sheet so small shapes don't overbake while large shapes take longer to fully bake.

Aspenglow

Prep 30 minutes **Chill** 30 minutes + 30 minutes **Bake** 8 minutes per batch **Cool** 5 minutes per batch
Decorating 50 minutes **Oven** 350°F **Makes** 22 medium cookies

COOKIES

1	package (14.5 ounces) gingerbread cake and cookie mix, *Betty Crocker*®
1/3	cup all-purpose flour
1/4	cup hot brewed double-strength decaf coffee, *Folgers*®
2	tablespoons butter, melted
1	tablespoon molasses, *Grandma's*®
1/4	teaspoon ground black pepper

ROYAL ICING

3	cups powdered sugar, sifted, *Domino*®/*C&H*®
2	teaspoons frozen lemon juice, thawed, *Minute Maid*®
1/3	cup refrigerated liquid egg whites, *All Whites*®

DECORATIONS

Clear sanding sugar

Colored decorating icings, *Cake Mate*® *Easy Squeeze* or *Betty Crocker*® *Easy Flow*

Colored decorating gels, *Cake Mate*®

Dragées** and/or tiny candies

My favorite holiday song is "Aspenglow" by John Denver. It has a beautiful melody and lyrics about friendship and laughter, peace, and how lovely the mountains are during this magical time of year.

1. For cookies, in a large bowl, stir together cookie mix and flour. Add coffee, butter, molasses, and pepper, stirring until well mixed. Shape dough into a ball; flatten into a disk. Wrap disk in plastic wrap. Chill in refrigerator for at least 30 minutes.

2. Line cookie sheets with parchment paper; set aside. On a lightly floured surface, roll out chilled dough to 1/4-inch thickness. Using holiday cookie cutters, cut out various shapes. Reroll scrap dough to cut out more shapes. Transfer same-size cookies to prepared cookie sheets, spacing cookies 2 inches apart.* Chill cutout cookies in refrigerator for at least 30 minutes.

3. Preheat oven to 350°F. Bake cookies for 8 to 10 minutes (depending on size) or just until set in centers. Cool on cookie sheets for 5 minutes. Transfer cookies to a wire rack; cool completely.

4. For royal icing, sift powdered sugar into a large mixing bowl. Add lemon juice. Gradually add egg whites, beating with electric mixer on medium until glossy. Beat in additional powdered sugar or egg whites to make desired consistency. If desired, dip one side of cooled cookies into royal icing or frost cookies with royal icing. Place cookies, iced sides up, on wire rack; let stand until icing hardens.

5. Meanwhile, spoon the remaining royal icing into a disposable piping bag; set aside. Snip a small piece off the end of the piping bag. Decorate cookie shapes with piped icing. Decorate with sanding sugar, decorating icing, decorating gels, dragées,** and/or tiny candies.

*Note: Arrange same-size cookies together on cookie sheet so small shapes don't overbake while large shapes take longer to fully bake.

**Note: Remove and discard dragées before eating cookies.

Index

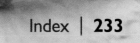

your personal back stage pass to
everything Sandra Lee
Follow her on Facebook + Twitter

Join in the fun at facebook.com/SandraLee

Follow Sandra @sandrashm (twitter.com/sandrashm)

Join Sandra on her Facebook page to interact and communicate with Sandra, her team, and other fans like you. Sandra posts frequently and you can receive recipes, videos of her cooking demonstrations, and behind-the-scene views of the making of her TV shows, "Sandra Lee's Semi-Homemade Cooking" and "Money Saving Meals" which air on Food Network. You can get in the action too—Sandra encourages you to post your comments and upload photos that show off your Semi-Homemade recipe masterpieces. Join now at facebook.com/sandralee.

Get up-to-the-minute insights from Sandra as she tweets about her life, travels, events, the making of her TV shows, books and magazines, and more!

Be the first to know—follow Sandra now on her Twitter page!

Join Sandra's Semi-Homemakers Club today at SandraLee.com!

the dynamic, interactive
SandraLee.com
will make your life better, easier and more enjoyable

Free Recipes

The official website for all things Sandra Lee

- New, exclusive recipes
- Read Sandra's BLOG
- A free subscription to the Semi-Homemakers Club eNewsletter
- Tons of terrific tablescapes
- Sandra's daily inspirational quote
- Q&A with Sandra
- And much more!

Enjoy the benefits of the
Semi-Homemade family today
at SandraLee.com!

sandra lee
Semi-Homemade®
MAGAZINE

Now you can have **over 450 recipes**
delivered right to your door!

Missed an Issue?

Feb/March 2009	April/May 2009	Dec/Jan 2010	May/ June 2010	July/Aug 2010
Sept/Oct 2010	Nov/Dec 2010	Halloween 2010	Christmas 2010	Jan/Feb 2011

Name _____

Address _____

City _____ State ____ Zip _____

Phone _____

E-mail _____

Return completed form to:
Sandra Lee Semi-Homemade Back Issues
1900 International Park Drive, Suite 50
Birmingham, AL 35243

Visit us online at
www.semihomemademag.com

Quantity

_____	Feb/March 2009	($4.99)
_____	April/May 2009	($4.99)
_____	Dec/Jan 2010	($4.99)
_____	May/June 2010	($4.99)
_____	July/Aug 2010	($4.99)
_____	Sept/Oct 2010	($4.99)
_____	Nov/Dec 2010	($4.99)
_____	Jan/Feb 2011	($4.99)
_____	Halloween 2010	($7.99)
_____	Christmas 2010	($7.99)

Total Quantity   Product Total   S&H   Total
_____ + _____ + _____ = _____

*AL, GA, IL, and NY residents add applicable sales tax.

Payment Method

☐ Check (payable to Sandra Lee Semi-Homemade)
☐ Visa   ☐ Mastercard

Card #:_____

Exp. Date_____ Signature _____

*Shipping and Handling		
(to one address)		
ISSUES	USA	CAN	FOR
1	$3.25	$3.25	$4.00
2-4	4.25	5.25	12.00
5-8	5.75	7.50	20.00
9-12	7.25	9.00	30.00
13-20	10.00	12.00	40.00
21-35	15.00	17.50	45.00
Pay in U.S. funds only.			
Allow 4-6 weeks for delivery!			

Sandra Lee
semi-homemade

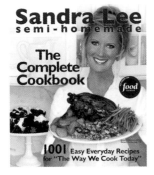

The Complete Cookbook

1001 Easy Everyday Recipes for "The Way We Cook Today"

Collect all of these smart, helpful, time- and money-saving books by best-selling author and Food Network star, Sandra Lee.

SANDRA LEE

MADE FROM SCRATCH
A Memoir